The
Future of
History

The Future of History

HISTORIANS, HISTORICAL ORGANIZATIONS,
AND THE PROSPECTS FOR THE FIELD

Conrad Edick Wright & Katheryn P. Viens,
editors

Published by the Massachusetts Historical Society,
Boston 2017

Massachusetts
Historical Society | **225**
1791–2016

Designed by Ondine Le Blanc

Library of Congress Cataloging-in-Publication Data
Names: Wright, Conrad Edick, editor of compilation. | Viens, Katheryn P.,
    1962- editor of compilation.
Title: The future of history : historians, historical organizations, and
    prospects for the field / Conrad Edick Wright and Katheryn P. Viens,
    editors.
Other titles: Historians, historical organizations, and prospects for the
    field
Description: Boston : Massachusetts Historical Society, [2017] | Includes
    bibliographical references.
Identifiers: LCCN 2017019926 | ISBN 9781936520114 (pbk.)
Subjects: LCSH: History--Study and teaching. | Historians. |
    History--Societies, etc.
Classification: LCC D16.2 .F87 2017 | DDC 907.1--dc23
LC record available at https://lccn.loc.gov/2017019926

Digital editions of this title are available
at the MHS website.

www.masshist.org/publications/future_history

The Future of History

HISTORIANS,

HISTORICAL ORGANIZATIONS,

AND THE PROSPECTS

FOR THE FIELD

Katheryn P. Viens

Introduction: Finding Meaning in the Past

ON MARCH 31, 2017, *PBS Newshour* aired an interview with Coron Bentley, an African American, Detroit autoworker who voiced his approval of President Trump's economic policies. As he told correspondent William Brangham, "There was talk of [Ford's] building a brand-new $700 million plant in Mexico, but, instead, they decided to invest that money in the plant that I work at. As Herbert Hoover once said, of all people, prosperity is right around the corner."[1] He gave a wry laugh.

Bentley was optimistic that, *this time*, renewed prosperity awaited all Americans, and he ironically quoted the president whose policies were most implicated in deepening the Great Depression. Through the historical allusion, Bentley compared the present economic moment to the past while demonstrating his belief in the magnitude of ongoing positive change. He shared his thoughts from the wooden bench of a picnic table in an urban neighborhood park, with a playing field and soccer net visible in the background.

A sense of history pervades American society, and it shows few signs of waning. Yet if this is the case, then why do many historians ex-

Katheryn P. Viens is the Director of Research at the Massachusetts Historical Society. She formerly served as Executive Director of the New England Museum Association, the region's professional organization for the field, and of the Old Colony Historical Society in Massachusetts. She has co-edited five essay collections and is the author of several scholarly articles. She is currently a PhD candidate in the American and New England Studies Program at Boston University.

press alarm about the "fate" or "future" of history? Are these concerns warranted? Answering this question involves not only training our eyes on how history is being recalled, used, and enjoyed—and where, from university podiums and city playing fields alike. It also involves turning our attention to those who issue the warnings and asking if the history they would preserve is the history they see around them.

In its simplest forms, history is both the practice of recovering the past and the thing that has been recalled: the birth, election, invention, tragedy, or triumph as it lives today in an image, artifact, document, or conversation. The past is all around us in the physical landscape of public monuments, libraries, and museums. It is also present in personal spaces—for example, at the kitchen doorjamb where pencil marks measure the growth of children long since moved away. It lives in scrapbooks and digital photo frames; in books and blogs, podcasts and websites; in live re-enactments, films, and video games set in historic moments. It lives in Congress and in classrooms. In society, history is ubiquitous and idiosyncratic.

In this modern environment, those who earn a living in the field are distinctly divided. We could all just wade into this historical universe and bathe ourselves in the riches of the past wherever they occur. Instead, half of us are standing on the riverbank, fretting about the depth, the cold, and the choppy water, and aiming to throw a life preserver to our peers. Meanwhile, many of us in the water quickly find ourselves exhausted.

As a field, we first need to make sense of this universe, to give order to the range of products and activities that history comprises, so that we can understand their significance and how we might respond. Too often, we categorize historical activities, including those we are in the process of developing ourselves, by the audiences they attract. Gaming is for teens and twenty-somethings. To develop a genealogy workshop, multiply the average age by three. This approach, however, leaves too many questions unanswered, including this: Why do many historical activities typically attract audiences that cut across age, gender, class, and racial lines? A more useful approach is to consider the role of history in people's lives, nothing more, nothing less. If we ask of each history activity we encounter, "How are people of various ages using this history lesson in its current form and content?" and "What purpose does it serve?" we will come to know its value for the millions of Americans, like Coron Bentley, who engage with history every day.

This approach allows us to organize historical activity according to its capacity to meet at least four basic human needs: to understand who we are as individuals and where we came from, to be part of a strong and vibrant community, to obtain respite, and to engage in civic life. All of us work to attain these things to varying degrees. Yet to satisfy our needs, it is not sufficient to call up the past or to enshrine it. Meeting these goals requires a deeper historical understanding.

Finding meaning in the past is the essential activity for achieving self-awareness and a life that is in balance, building healthy communities, and forming a just and equitable civic society. We uncover the sacrifices our ancestors made to obtain an education, and the knowledge shapes our own work ethic. We learn of discrimination and violence that occurred in a prior era, and we discover lessons that help us make our present-day community a safe and friendly place. We study past decisions and find the proper means to address modern policy challenges. To find meaning in the past is, essentially, to build a bridge between then and now.

Professional historians—not all of whom are academics!—are among those who best know how this process works. Whether they carry out their research and teaching in a university, museum, research library, secondary school, editorial project, or another setting, historians gain the experience of years of training, practice, and peer review. This process makes them uniquely qualified to apply a toolkit of foundational knowledge, research skills, and categories of analysis to tease meaning out of past events. When they express concern about the future of history, it is often because they are keenly aware of instances of missed insight where more accurate and useful meanings could be discovered from the past. At other times, they perceive an imbalance of priorities among individuals and communities that their knowledge of history teaches them is detrimental: the privileging of the self over community building or civic engagement, for example. They are also highly attuned to situations in which participants profess to be uninterested in the past or consider history to be of little relative value.

But who listens to historians anyway? Because the field demands extensive preparation, often including graduate study, historians attain a certain amount of cultural capital that this education provides. This places them in the company of policy makers, so-called "serious" journalists, and even comic social critics whose education in Arts and Letters has given them, too, a foundation in historical knowledge, critical thinking, and research skills. Too often these groups self-identify and are recognized as intellectual "elites," perched on the far side of a gulf that separates them from "ordinary" Americans who are visiting historic sites and reading, role-playing, and discussing history.

To ask whether or not ordinary Americans are capable of finding meaning in the past because we observe that many members of the public lack a formal education is a moot point: they are already doing so. In this environment, what is the responsibility of professional historians when they perceive that the resulting conclusions are incomplete or badly skewed? With the fate of individuals, communities, and civic order at stake, the matter is too important to let lie. In what ways will historians share their precious knowledge and skills? When we transfer this knowledge and these skills, are we divesting ourselves of social capital or developing a more widespread appreciation for our discipline? Or, might we be gaining currency in the form of knowledge and skills that inhere in non-academic settings among a more diverse population? In other words, what do historians stand to learn from history as ordinary Americans understand it?

These are among the challenging questions that the essayists in this volume address. The authors were among the more than fifty leaders in the field whom the Massachusetts Historical Society convened in September 2016 for a workshop entitled "The Future of History." One of our goals for this program was explicitly to break down barriers between academic and public historians, be they administrators, educators, or editors. With their chairs arranged in a large oval and with no breakout sessions, colleagues who don't ordinarily have an opportunity to engage one another discussed the connections between academic history and the history the public consumes, and whether we are doing the history we want to do. They considered the social costs of *not* doing history and where to find the next generation of practitioners and consumers. They pondered, "Does history matter?" while keeping in mind the prior evening's keynote address by Jonathan F. Fanton, the president of the American Academy of Arts and Sciences, who declared his confidence in the title of his talk, "The Past Has a Future."[2]

The present volume aims to continue this conversation. We begin by examining the opportunities that exist to use history to shape our world and, moreover, to frame the historical narrative itself. As John Stauffer observes, those for whom history is "the activist's muse" are part of a long tradition that includes historians who aimed to influence society, politics, and the economy through their work. Richard Rabinowitz celebrates the ways in which audiences today seize the opportunity to shape how history museums present the past and the stories they tell by engaging staff members in lively discussions and experiential learning. Paul J. Erickson offers historians the breadth of the Internet as a space for conducting research, refining our thoughts, and engaging with an expansive community that is writing its own history online.

Various challenges impede historians' efforts and demand creative solutions. Louise Mirrer characterizes the strains on funding for both academic departments and historical organizations, which can inhibit even the largest institutions as they seek to fulfill their missions. Yet Gretchen Sullivan Sorin notes that history emanates from within the community, as neighborhood residents collaborate with local historical societies to reshape these institutions in fundamental ways to meet their needs. She calls upon historians to achieve this degree of diversity throughout their field. Debra Block urges K–12 educators and policy makers to follow the best examples in pedagogy and assessment to give students the knowledge and skills they will need in the twenty-first century. Among these are critical thinking: the ability to distinguish truth from falsehood while recognizing historical paradoxes and multiple points of view.

A college or university environment that imposes structural chal-lenges and inhibits the free exchange of ideas subverts the goal of his-torical understanding, as Manisha Sinha shows. At his university, John Lauritz Larson completely redesigned the American history course he teaches to reflect what his students told him are the most pressing concerns of their lives. (If you're wondering what these are, read the essay!) His decision was, in part, a response to the downturns in his-tory department registrations and job openings that Robert Townsend describes. Townsend analyzes this recurring phenomenon, considers how the current academic climate is different, and ponders whether the lessons learned will survive the next recovery. It is notable that among the responses is a push for courses that will prepare students to work in archives, museums, and other public history settings. As a recent study showed, acquiring the right combination of skills and experience is essential for students who wish to work in public history, a field that is itself still recovering from the recession of 2008.[3]

The environment in which the next generation will make its mark is rapidly changing. Stephen A. Marini considers the most recent shifts in how the public at large receives information and discerns truth, calling out those who trade in relativism and alternative facts. In this evolving cultural context, public historical organizations find that sup-port for their work continues to vary in degree and in kind. Ellsworth H. Brown weighs how institutions assess the benefits and pitfalls of various forms of public and private funding and strategically deploy them in serving the public. Marilynn S. Johnson shows us how, in the context of departmental cuts, college and university history classrooms are preparing students to make vital contributions to the workforce and society more broadly, using critical thinking, collaborative tech-niques, and the ability to optimize new media.

Should there still be any question concerning the extent of the chal-lenges the field of history faces, the strength of our resolve, or the scale of the achievements we are poised to make, we end with essays that tackle the question of "owning" history head on. In the experience of Cinnamon Catlin-Legutko, historical institutions are providing model spaces that undo centuries of colonizing practices and promote mutual understanding among diverse racial and ethnic groups. Dennis A. Fiori takes a close look at the controversial practice of merging what are often small, community-based organizations, which can eliminate the duplication of efforts, build organizational capacity, and increase support in the long run.

The practice of history calls on all of us to maintain a clear understanding of the importance of history in our society, work ceaselessly to overcome the challenges that face the field, and maintain our readiness to adapt to critical changes that will most certainly occur in the years ahead. History is not merely about acquiring a body of knowledge—although it is arguably more difficult to be a contributing member of society without knowing the significance of Rosa Parks, or Auschwitz, or the eleventh hour on the eleventh day of the eleventh month, 1918.

Think about the anecdote that began this introduction. Do you remember the name of the man interviewed by PBS? Mr. Bentley's surname appeared four times in this essay, and his first name, Coron, twice. Do you recall the date on which the interview aired? Perhaps you only remember a middle-aged black man in a Detroit park, with faith in the political process and a bright vision of America's future based on his knowledge of history. For now, that is enough.

1 Coron Bentley interview with correspondent William Brangham, "Trump Supporters in Michigan Confident Their Votes Will Pay Off," *PBS Newshour*, March 31, 2017, www.pbs.org/newshour/bb/trump-supporters-michigan-confident-votes-will-pay-off.

2 This address may be viewed on the Massachusetts Historical Society's YouTube channel at www.youtube.com/watch?v=UxTQtOYKyRY.

3 Philip Scarpino and Daniel Vivian, "What Do Public History Employers Want? Report of the Joint AASLH-AHA-NCPH-OAH Task Force on Public History Education and Employment" (2015).

John Stauffer   History Is the Activist's Muse

"U.S.A. is . . . a publiclibrary full of old newspapers and dogeared histo-rybooks with protests scrawled on the margins in pencil."

—John Dos Passos, *U.S.A.* (1937)

"'Who controls the past,' ran the Party slogan, 'controls the future: who controls the present controls the past.' . . . All history was a palimpsest, scraped clean and reinscribed exactly as often as was necessary. In no case would it have been possible, once the deed was done, to prove that any falsification had taken place."

—George Orwell, *Nineteen Eighty-Four* (1949)

"A keen sense of history begets a feeling of social responsibility and a need to act."

—Richard Hofstadter, *The Progressive Historians* (1968)

"[The black scholar] has to be like any other scholar in his field, but he must also be an advocate for justice and equality so he can be heard as a scholar and survive as a human being."

—John Hope Franklin, Interview (1973)

John Stauffer is Professor of English and African and African American studies at Harvard University and the author or editor of twenty books, including *The Black Hearts of Men*, *GIANTS*, and *Picturing Frederick Douglass*. He has long been interested in the relationship between activism, art, and history.

"The necessity of history is deeply rooted in personal psychic need and in the human striving for community. None can testify better to this necessity than members of groups who have been denied a usable past. . . . Quite naturally each of these groups, as it moved closer to a position of sharing power with those ruling society, has asserted its claim to the past."

—Gerda Lerner, "The Necessity of History
and the Professional Historian" (1982)

"Expelled from individual consciousness by the rush of change, history finds its revenge by stamping the collective unconscious with habits, values, expectations, dreams. The dialectic between past and present will continue to shape our lives."

—Arthur M. Schlesinger, Jr., *The Cycles of American History* (1986)[1]

W. E. B. DU BOIS WAS keenly aware of historians' efforts to use the past as a means to shape the future. In the last chapter of his *Black Reconstruction in America* (1935), he excoriated them for ignoring or changing facts about the Civil War era in order to defend white supremacy and Jim Crow segregation. The treatment of the era reflected "small credit upon American historians as scientists" or "artists using the results of science," he wrote, at a time when many historians imagined themselves as scientists.[2]

The war had left "terrible wounds" that needed to be healed: "The South was ashamed because it fought to perpetuate human slavery. The North was ashamed because it had to call in the black men to save the Union, abolish slavery and establish democracy." In their efforts to heal these wounds, historians became activists for the South, ignoring the evils of slavery and the humanity of blacks. They deliberately "changed the facts of history" so that the story would "make pleasant reading for Americans. . . . In the end nobody seems to have done wrong and everybody was right." According to the historians, Confederate soldiers "died fighting for liberty."[3]

The purpose of history was to "guide humanity," Du Bois wrote. The past could be a vital tool for reformers and activists, who also sought to guide humanity and recognized that one's understanding of the past informed the present and influenced the future. But historians needed to be honest in acknowledging the sins of the past. All nations "reel and stagger on their way; they make hideous mistakes; they commit frightful wrongs; they do great and beautiful things." Historians had an obligation "to tell the truth" about society's vices as well as its virtues, "so far as the truth is ascertainable."[4] Only then might people find a way to avoid repeating the sins of the past. Only then could progress occur. Only then could humanity become more humane.

Du Bois saw no contradiction or tension between history, activism, and empiricism as long as one "told the truth." Telling the truth meant that one needed to be faithful to the sources and avoid cherry-picking them, whether out of laziness, inconvenience, or a preconceived argument that aligned with worthy visions for the future.[5] His PhD advisor at Harvard, the historian Albert Bushnell Hart, was the son of abolitionists and, like Du Bois, a meticulous researcher and moralist, who had "drummed into his students the sanctity of primary sources and of careful scrutiny of documents."[6]

But the historians Du Bois rebuked in *Black Reconstruction* ignored or distorted the facts while defining their scholarship (at least publicly) as "dispassionate." In their rhetoric and tone, they pretended to be uninterested in using the past to shape the future, thus publicly denying their agenda of defending white supremacy and black unfreedom. These historians were some of the most prominent scholars of the era: William Dunning, John Burgess, Ulrich B. Phillips, and Frederick Jackson Turner.[7] In Du Bois's reckoning, they resembled the historians in George Orwell's *Nineteen Eighty-Four*, in which history became "a palimpsest, scraped clean and reinscribed exactly as often as was necessary" to sustain the "closed society," or totalitarian state.[8]

ACTIVISTS HAVE LONG USED HISTORY as a muse or means to "set the world right," as Du Bois phrased it, and realize their vision of a better society.[9] But scholars have only recently acknowledged the intimate links between the past and the future, between history and activism. For much of the twentieth century, Americanists argued that activists were comparatively ignorant of history. In the past decade, however, Zoe Trodd and other scholars have debunked the myth of American reformers and their movements as a series of "fresh starts" and new beginnings. Instead, they draw attention to the inspiration and influence that history—whether in the form of books, archives, museums, or monuments—has had on activists.[10] Socialists and Wobblies referred to themselves as the new abolitionists; Civil Rights activists defined their movement as the Second Reconstruction; and second-wave feminists identified with the abolition and Civil Rights movements.[11] Moreover, abolitionists, Confederates, African Americans, feminists, labor activists, and environmentalists all wrote the first histories of their respective groups and movements.[12] They created a "usable past" for understanding the present and shaping the future. Gerda Lerner explains this phenomenon: "The necessity of history is deeply rooted in personal psychic need and in the human striving for community. None can testify better to this necessity than members of groups who have been denied a usable past."[13] These groups seek to recover a usable past that can inform their present and shape their future.

Academic historians have often been *publicly* uncomfortable acknowledging the "dialectic" between past, present, and future, as Arthur M. Schlesinger, Jr., phrased it, and thus their role as activists.[14] They often seem unaware of the long-standing tradition of scholars explicitly linking past and present. For decades the notion that a scholar's work should be "dispassionate" was something of a mantra in many departments. It was as if dispassionate rhetoric and a detached tone reflected devotion to empirical research and especially to the past solely for its own sake, regardless of how careful the practitioners were in "telling the truth" about the sources, as Du Bois phrased it.[15]

In their *private* correspondence, however, scholars have often revealed their activist missions and passions. Frank Owsley, in a letter to his friend and fellow Southerner Allen Tate, described how he used the rhetoric and tone of detachment to further his activist mission of redeeming the South: "The purpose of my life is to undermine by 'careful' and 'detached,' 'well documented,' 'objective' writing, the entire Northern myth [of antislavery and moral uprightness] from 1820 to 1876."[16]

Owsley's letter betrays an honesty about his activism that is obscured in the dispassionate tone of his presidential address to the Southern Historical Society in 1940. In this influential essay, he argued that "egocentric sectionalism" among Northerners and Southerners was the central cause of the Civil War. His evidence for Northern egocentrism is the abolitionists. They were moral absolutists, he argues, and he likens them to totalitarian Nazis and Communists: "as far as I have been able to ascertain, neither Dr. Goebbels nor Virginio Gayda nor Stalin's propaganda agents have as yet been able to plumb the depths of vulgarity and obscenity reached and maintained by . . . Stephen Foster, Wendell Phillips, Charles Sumner, and other abolitionists of note." Owsley states this as a fact and scholarly interpretation, while ignoring the abolitionists' devotion to civil rights and human rights and their frequent collaborations with conservative antislavery advocates.[17]

In another private letter, C. Vann Woodward explained how the rhetoric and tone of detachment could further the activist mission of redeeming the South. After his friend and fellow Southerner David Donald won the Pulitzer Prize for *Charles Sumner and the Coming of the Civil War* (1960), Woodward applauded Donald's "deadpan" tone while ignoring his manipulation of the sources.[18] Donald had used the perfect form to mask his vilification of a leading abolitionist. As Woodward shrewdly noted in a letter to Robert Penn Warren, "I think Donald's dead-panning of Sumner is just about right. How can anybody pretend about this joker [Sumner] any more. But they will!"[19]

In yet another letter among Southerners, in 1929 Allen Tate spelled out his activist mission to Donald Davidson.[20] Tate outlined a plan for creating "a society or an academy of Southern positive reactionaries," based on the "prototype" of the "old South"—an organic, agrarian society that would offer "a complete social, philosophical, literary, economic, and religious system." It was a mission aimed at combatting corporate capitalism and redeeming the South. "We should be *secretive*," Tate emphasized, "in our tactics." His blueprint was partly successful; by the middle decades of the twentieth century, a "potent, pro-Southern bias" dominated American history and literary scholarship, according to Hugh Tulloch.[21]

Southerners were not the only ones to betray a passionate, activist bias in their private letters. In 1946, Kenneth Stampp ranted to his mentor, William Hesseltine, about prominent racist "doughface" and Southern historians: "James G. Randall is a damned Negro-hating, abolitionist-baiting, doughface. . . . I'm sick of the Randalls, Cravens and other doughfaces who crucify the abolitionists for attacking slavery. If I had lived in the 1850s, I would have been a rabid abolitionist. . . . My only criticism of the Radicals is that they weren't radical enough, at least so far as the southern problem was concerned."[22]

Ten years later, Stampp published *The Peculiar Institution* (1956), the first twentieth-century history from a white American that overturned the characterization of slavery as a benign institution. Stampp relied heavily on testimony from slaves and ex-slaves, recast slavery as a state of war, and emphasized the resistance and agency of blacks. He wrote as an activist and acknowledged his biases. His work inspired a new generation of scholars, including David Brion Davis's trilogy, *The Problem of Slavery*.[23]

Scholars' letters often betray not only their biases but their activism—their desire to link the past to the present and future. Indeed one could conclude from their correspondence in the early and middle decades of the twentieth century that they were still fighting the Civil War, at least ideologically. When E. Merton Coulter published *The South During Reconstruction* (1947), Harry T. Williams bemoaned the glowing reviews "of Coulter's godawful book. . . . Isn't someone going to have the courage to say it's based on race prejudice and distortion of the sources?" John Hope Franklin answered Williams's call: he published a scathing review of Coulter's book in the *Journal of Negro History* and, knowing that few white historians read the journal regularly, sent five hundred reprints "to historians all over the country," as Franklin noted. "The response was tremendous."[24]

Among the many insights in Peter Novick's magisterial book, *That Noble Dream*, is the degree to which historians have so often cloaked their activism in the guise of scholarly detachment, or "objectivity." As Novick notes, objectivity has been understood more as a matter of form, of tone and rhetoric, than in the use of sources, coupled with a Whiggish understanding of history, in which each new generation of scholarship gets closer to the truth.[25] But the idea of progress in the historiography of the Civil War era is absurd. The first histories by white and black historians—Henry Wilson, Hermann Von Holst, George Washington Williams, Du Bois, Joseph T. Wilson, and Carter Woodson—more closely resonate with the tone and substance of recent scholarship on abolitionism and blacks' role in the conflict than most of the work published in the twentieth century.[26]

Novick also reveals the long tradition, influence, and popularity of activist historians, from Charles Beard and Carl Becker through John Hope Franklin, Arthur Schlesinger, Jr., and Gerda Lerner. For much of the twentieth century, Novick notes, historians were quite comfortable with betraying their activism by linking the past with the present and future. Becker and Beard were among the most influential historians of the twentieth century. Their presidential addresses to the American Historical Association in 1932 (Becker) and 1934 (Beard) continue to be cited and discussed. As Novick explains, "No belief was more central to [them] than that history existed for man, not man for history. The historian's social responsibility was to provide an account of the past appropriate to society's current needs."[27] Beard and Becker promoted their activism.

Becker believed that everyone was his or her own historian, connecting the past to his or her own present needs. He anticipated the recent transformation in American history, in which groups that had been denied a usable past, such as women, blacks, and Native Americans, have asserted their claims to the past, leading Novick to characterize the profession in the past forty years as "every group its own historian."[28]

Beard argued that history was "an act of faith" based on one's conception of progress; "the world moves," as he put it, either progressing or regressing. Beard acknowledged that he saw history moving "forward" to "a collectivist democracy." In interpreting how the world (or society) moved, the historian connected past with present and thus helped "to *make* history," rather than simply interpret the past for its own sake.[29]

Becker's and Beard's understanding of history empowered every individual to use the past as a means for shaping the present and future. Understandably, their work received wide popular and critical acclaim. In a *New Republic* symposium on the influence of scholars in 1938, Beard was ranked second after Thorstein Veblen, ahead of John Dewey and Sigmund Freud.[30]

It was only after World War II that the ethos of the "past for its own sake" began to flourish. Historians were expected to "totally disengage themselves" from present-day assumptions and concerns to avoid historical anachronisms. It was as though the profession was trying to isolate variables in order to study the past like a scientist. Herbert Butterfield's *Whig Interpretation of History* (1931), which argued that history progressed, always getting closer to truth, became "a staple of postwar reading lists." It was an extraordinary shift in how history was understood. Indeed, from the founding of the American Historical Association in 1884 until 1945, presidential addresses had emphasized the importance of studying the past for the sake of the present.[31]

The shift to analyzing the past for its own sake coincided with an inward turn (or navel-gazing) in the profession, in which historians abandoned their previous aspirations to write for a general audience. Instead, they directed their work to a "strictly academic" audience. Historians now felt free to say "the public be damned." Not surprisingly, the popularity of history among the general public declined dramatically.[32]

The pressure to study the past for its own sake became so pervasive that even such prominent activist historians as Arthur Schlesinger, Jr., who won two Pulitzer Prizes, served as a presidential advisor to John F. Kennedy, and had always emphasized the degree to which the past and present would shape our futures, felt compelled to chant, with a straight face, the mantra that history should be studied only for its own sake.[33]

Yet as Schlesinger and most historians from the founding of the profession had recognized, history was meaningful to society only when it resonated with the present, serving as a muse for one's vision of the future. Such an approach to the past had energized history and the humanities. Perhaps it could again. "All human beings are practicing historians," Gerda Lerner notes. "We live our lives; we tell our stories. It is as natural as breathing."[34] History preserves these stories, making them resonant and relevant.

Such resonance can be achieved without sacrificing the craft of doing history. Gerda Lerner, Arthur Schlesinger, Jr., John Hope Franklin, Richard Hofstadter, W. E. B. Du Bois, and countless other activist historians recognized that their scholarly rigor needed to be at least as good as that of historians who sought to interpret the past for its own sake. But they also recognized that the very topic a historian chooses to write about is, whether they acknowledge it or not, a decision that has social, political, emotional, and often spiritual, as well as scholarly and intellectual, implications.[35]

1 John Dos Passos, preface to *U.S.A.: The 42nd Parallel* (1937; Boston, 1946), viii–ix; George Orwell, *Nineteen Eighty-Four* (1949; New York, 2003), 35–36, 41; Richard Hofstadter, *The Progressive Historians: Turner, Beard, Parrington* (New York, 1968), 465–466; F. Holden, "John Hope Franklin, Scholar," *University of Chicago Magazine,* Sept. 1980, p. 17; Gerda Lerner, "The Necessity of History and the Professional Historian" (presidential address to the Organization of American Historians), *Journal of American History* 69(1982):11–12; Arthur M. Schlesinger, Jr., *The Cycles of American History* (Boston, 1986), xiii.

2 W. E. B. Du Bois, "The Propaganda of History," *Writings,* ed. Nathan Huggins (New York, 1986), 1028, 1029.

3 Du Bois, "The Propaganda of History," 1026, 1028–1029, 1030, 1031.

4 Du Bois, "The Propaganda of History," 1030.

5 I am indebted to Conrad E. Wright for this sentence. Conrad Edick Wright to John Stauffer, April 9, 2017, email.

6 David Levering Lewis, *W. E. B. Du Bois: Biography of a Race, 1868–1919* (New York, 1993), 112 (quotation), 383; David Levering Lewis, introduction to W. E. B. Du Bois, *Black Reconstruction in America, 1860–1880* (1935; New York, 1998), vii–xvii.

Hart openly acknowledged that he was the son of abolitionists. In his preface to *Slavery and Abolition*, he noted that it had been difficult to "approach so explosive a question with impartiality." See Alfred Bushnell Hart, *Slavery and Abolition, 1831–1841* (New York, 1906), xv.

7 Du Bois, "Propaganda of History," 1028, 1035, 1038.

8 Orwell, *Nineteen Eighty-Four*, 41.

9 Du Bois, "Criteria of Negro Art" (1926), *Writings*, 995.

10 John Stauffer, foreword to *American Protest Literature*, ed. Zoe Trodd (Cambridge, Mass., 2006), xi.

11 Trodd, ed., *American Protest Literature*, xx–xxiii, 116, 118; John Stauffer and Benjamin Soskis, *The Battle Hymn of the Republic: A Biography of the Song That Marches On* (New York, 2013), 179, 201–202.

12 Robert P. Forbes, "'Truth Systematised': The Changing Debate over Slavery and Abolition, 1761–1916," and Manisha Sinha, "Coming of Age: The Historiography of Black Abolitionism," in *Prophets of Protest: Reconsidering the History of American Abolitionism*, ed. Timothy Patrick McCarthy and John Stauffer (New York, 2006), 3–22, 23–24, 30; William Cooper Nell, *The Colored Patriots of the American Revolution* (Boston, 1855); George Washington Williams, *A History of the Negro Race in America from 1619 to 1880: Negroes as Slaves, as Soldiers, and as Citizens* (New York, 1888); Thomas J. Pressly, *Americans Interpret Their Civil War* (Princeton, 1954), 73–95; Elizabeth Cady Stanton, Susan B. Anthony, Matilda Joslyn Gage, and Ida Husted Harper, eds., *History of Woman Suffrage* (Rochester and New York, 1881–1922); Alice Clark, *Working Life of Women in the Seventeenth Century* (London, 1919); Barbara Drake, *Women and Trade Unions* (London, 1920); Barbara L. Hutchins, *Women in Modern Industry* (London, 1915); Greg Kucich, "Women's Historiography and the (dis) Embodiment of Law: Ann Yearsley, Mary Hays, Elizabeth Benger," *Wordsworth Circle* 33(2002):3–7; Thomas A. Krueger, "American Labor Historiography, Old and New," *Journal of Social History* 4(1971):277–285; Leonard Krieger, "Marx and Engels as Historians," *Journal of the History of Ideas* 14(1953):381–403.

13 Lerner, "Necessity of History," 11–12.

14 Schlesinger, *Cycles of American History*, xiii.

15 Du Bois, "Criteria of Negro Art," 995.

16 Frank Owsley, quoted in Peter Novick, *That Noble Dream: The "Objectivity Question" and the American Historical Profession* (Cambridge, 1988), 238.

17 Frank L. Owsley, "The Fundamental Cause of the Civil War: Egocentric Sectionalism," *Journal of Southern History* 7(1941):3–18 (quotation 16). On the abolitionists' frequent collaborations with conservative antislavery advocates, see John Stauffer,

"The Union of Abolitionists and Emancipationists in Civil War–Era Massachusetts," in *Massachusetts and the Civil War: The Commonwealth and National Disunion*, ed. Matthew Mason, Katheryn P. Viens, and Conrad Edick Wright (Amherst, Mass., 2015), 9–46.

18 On Donald's manipulation of his sources, see Louis Ruchames, "The Pulitzer Prize Treatment of Charles Sumner," *Massachusetts Review* 2(1961):749–769; and Gilbert Osofsky, "Cardboard Yankee: How Not to Study the Mind of Charles Sumner," *Reviews in American History* 1(1973):595–606.

19 Woodward to Warren, Sept. 26, 1960, Robert Penn Warren Papers, YCAL MSS 51, Box 82, Sterling Library, Yale University.

20 Although Tate is best known as a rigorous, "scientific" New Critic, his first book was an influential biography of Stonewall Jackson.

21 Allen Tate to Donald Davidson, Aug. 10, 1929, in *The Literary Correspondence of Donald Davidson and Allen Tate*, ed. John Tyree Fain and Thomas Daniel Young (Athens, Ga., 1974), 229–230; Hugh Tulloch, *The Debate on the American Civil War Era* (Manchester, 1999), 10; Mark Jancovich, *The Cultural Politics of the New Criticism* (Cambridge, 1993); Jancovich, "The Southern New Critics," in *The Cambridge History of Literary Criticism*, vol. 7: *Modernism and the New Criticism*, ed. A. Walton Litz, Louis Menand, and Lawrence Rainey (Cambridge, 2000), 200–218; John Stauffer, "Literary Neo-Confederates and Civil Rights," *Modern Language Studies* 39(2009):42–55.

22 Kenneth Stampp to William Hesseltine, March 6, 1946, quoted in Novick, *That Noble Dream*, 349.

23 David Brion Davis, *The Problem of Slavery in the Age of Emancipation* (New York, 2014), xi–xii.

24 Harry T. Williams and John Hope Franklin, quoted in Novick, *That Noble Dream*, 349n; Jacqueline Goggin, "Countering White Racist Scholarship: Carter G. Woodson and *The Journal of Negro History*," *Journal of Negro History* 68(1983):355–375.

25 Novick, *That Noble Dream*, 13–84, 226–260, 274–333, 341–383, 479–541.

26 Pressly, *Americans Interpret Their Civil War*, vii–xv; Stauffer, "Union of Abolitionists and Emancipationists," 12–16; David W. Blight, *Race and Reunion: The Civil War in American Memory* (Cambridge, Mass., 2001). In his 1962 paperback edition of *Americans Interpret Their Civil War*, Pressly acknowledged that his book had not "provide[d] much warmth for the ego of the historian" wedded to an objective, Whiggish understanding of the past. Contemporaries "interpreted the crises of their age with as much understanding as has been mustered by trained historians of later generations." See Novick, *That Noble Dream*, 360.

27 Novick, *That Noble Dream*, 250–278 (quotation 255).

28 Novick, *That Noble Dream*, 256, 469–521 (quotation 469); Eric Foner, introduction to Steven Hahn, *A Nation without Borders: The United States and Its World in An Age of Civil Wars, 1830–1910* (New York, 2016), ix–x; Carl Becker, "Everyman His Own Historian," *American Historical Review* 37(1932):221–236.

29 Charles A. Beard, "Written History as an Act of Faith," *American Historical Review* 39(1934):228 (emphasis added).

30 Novick, *That Noble Dream*, 240, 258.

31 Novick, *That Noble Dream*, 372–375 (quotations 374, 375).

32 Novick, *That Noble Dream*, 373, 374.

33 Novick, *That Noble Dream*, 374, 376; Schlesinger, *Cycles of American History*, xiii. See also Schlesinger, Jr., "Introduction to the Transaction Edition," *The Vital Center: The Politics of Freedom* (1949; New Brunswick, 1998), ix–xviii.

34 Gerda Lerner, *Why History Matters* (New York, 1997), 199.

35 I am indebted to Conrad E. Wright for this last paragraph. Conrad Edick Wright to John Stauffer, April 9, 2017, email.

Richard Rabinowitz

History in Every Sense: Public and Academic History

HOW SHALL WE COUNT the multitudinous types of historians? There are grey eminences holding down endowed chairs in major universities, and there are adjunct professors racing about to cover survey courses in a dozen neighboring institutions of higher learning. Historians and curators preside over great collections at our museums, libraries, and historical societies, and community activists scramble to record stories that have not yet been granted admission to those hallowed precincts. There are the hybrids—the professors who write op-ed pieces and others who lead community history projects. Everywhere, professional historians—K–12 classroom teachers, archivists, preservationists, members of memorial commissions, and curriculum developers; guidebook writers, long-form journalists, and authors of historical fiction, biography, and narrative nonfiction; performance artists, screenwriters of costume dramas, and website, game, and app developers—readjust our local narratives to suit new ideas about what is important to remember and tell. Beyond that, brigades of armchair historians, buffs, re-enactors, enthusiasts, and collectors survey the past in minute detail. And then there are the many of you, dear readers, who turn from the navel-gazing of contemporary fiction and

Richard Rabinowitz, President of American History Workshop in Brooklyn since 1980, has led creative teams in developing over five hundred public history projects, including new museums and exhibitions in thirty-four states and the District of Columbia. He is the author of the recently published *Curating America: Journeys through Storyscapes of the American Past* (2016).

seek to trace the end of the Ottoman Empire, or the beginning of the Manhattan Project, or something else definitively *real*. Ask Wikipedia a question about something that happened in the past and you're suddenly surrounded by a teeming throng of commentators.

Complain as we do about the State Of History Today, whoever it is who makes historians has been working overtime. Given this plenitude, we make a terrible mistake if we consider the tenured faculty in research universities as the norm in our historical thinking and practice. They represent, after all, only a very tiny fraction of the vast population of historians, even of those in full-time employment. Those of us who work as public historians chafe at the narrow-minded dismissal of our lot as second-class devotees of Clio. We are dismayed when foundations and research libraries, and even universities teaching public history, exclude practicing public historians from eligibility for summer seminars and research fellowships. We are thus astonished when universities, in their periodic perplexity about the job crisis in academe, ask us to advise students desperately seeking a "Plan B."

We have long been used to thinking of historical knowledge as if it were an industrial product. It is assumedly invented in laboratories (the study of the scholar), prototyped in factories (the seminar room), and then distributed through expanding orbits of popularization (from lecture hall to bookstore to exhibition galleries and television screens). In this narrative, the public historian is merely a distributor or disseminator of knowledge produced by the loftier types in the ivory tower. But in my own career I've seen how wrong-headed this is. To be sure, there is a difference between (1) history researched, written, and taught in the university and (2) history researched, represented, and brought to the general public through a variety of media. But, as I've tried to explain in my new book, *Curating America: Journeys through Storyscapes of the American Past*, both the academic historian and the public historian are in the business of discovery as well as dissemination. (In fact, so too is the public they address.) Over 50 years and through 560-plus projects, I have never embarked on a historical program without carving new inroads beyond the current scholarly terrain. Otherwise, why bother?

MY FRIENDS THOUGHT I'd gone mad when I took a leave from graduate school in 1967 to work as a costumed interpreter at Old Sturbridge Village (OSV). Strutting about in a silly looking broad-brimmed hat, high boots, and button-fly trousers, chatting up tourists and school-children with tidbits of New England history—that seemed less than dignified for a promising PhD candidate who'd once enjoyed the tute-lage of the august Perry Miller. But I soon found myself immersed in two challenges—scholarly and pedagogical—that transformed my idea of what it meant to be a historian.

First, the outdoor museum radically expanded what might be considered historical sources. When I welcomed visitors to the old schoolhouse at OSV, the building offered much more than the con-temporaneous writings of Noah Webster or Horace Mann on school-ing. Museum visitors sliding into desks long scarred by generations of penknife-wielding Candia, New Hampshire, children, could immerse themselves in the sounds and smells of the room. The visitors' fingers quickly learned how proximity to the room's little stove might affect their ability to hold a pencil or to warm legs in threadbare stockings. Their eyes could squint at old textbook pages through the dwindling light of winter afternoons. Museum-goers could imagine squirming to escape the glare of teachers and the threats of bullies. And they could, perhaps, absorb the information I could provide about the age range of pupils in such schools, the limits on what girls were taught, the length of the school year, and the bitter memories of schoolmasters and -mistresses about their stingy employers. What a toolbox for my teaching that room gave me!

Further, the visitors took none of this in passively. To a person, sixth-graders and venerable grandmothers alike took center stage to tell me about their own schooling experience, their philosophy of fam-ily discipline, and their feelings about experts and teachers. If they had been hushed in schoolrooms long ago, they certainly weren't about to be silenced now! I let all their comments and questions flow on, relinquishing my impulse to press upon them my own synthesis of the role of education in the forming of American society. It felt like an ongoing, collaborative seminar on educational history. At night, I took notes about what I could remember of the best anecdotes and the most fiercely expressed attitudes.

It was only when I returned to Harvard to complete my course-work and become a teaching fellow in history and literature that I understood how much I'd learned in this first stint in what I subsequently came to call "public history." The materials I could assign in my mini-seminar on American life-writing ranged from Anne Bradstreet's poetry to *The Autobiography of Malcolm X*, but it was all text all the time. And how could I charm these competitive college students into working together? What would induce them to hammer out a collaborative understanding of our readings instead of displaying their own self-proclaimed superior perspectives? They were being judged, after all, by their individual achievements and would be prized—everyone agreed—if they spoke with a clear, original, and singular voice. I missed the generous, collaborative spirit of informal learning in the museum. I could find almost no one with whom to think hard about pedagogy. For many colleagues, it seemed, curriculum design was no more than choosing the assigned readings, and a teacher's most profound responsibility was to red-pencil student papers ferociously.

As a place to teach American history, the museum was—hands down—the finer platform. I could engage my learners more intensively, bring more diverse sources and methods for them to explore, and learn more from their responses. So once I'd passed my PhD exams and the outdoor museum came calling again, I leapt at the opportunity to become the assistant director for interpretation and education at OSV in 1969.

Still, I always knew that I would go on to complete my dissertation and earn the doctoral degree, even though the credential wasn't necessary to make progress in the museum field. The research would mostly have to be done on weekends and the writing at night only, after very busy days in the museum. But I pressed on. Completing the thesis was evidence of the still-powerful attraction of the academic conversation I had so happily abandoned years before.

My dissertation explored the evolving personal experience of religion in nineteenth-century New England. For that research, I read dozens of diaries and memoirs, accounts of revivals, and other descriptions of how the minds of ordinary Christians grappled with the ultimate issues of redemption and salvation as New England rural life was transformed by economic development and social change. Of course, my day job meant I understood my historical souls as physical as well as intellectual beings, as people who chopped onions as well as logic.

The dissertation, and the book that came from it (*The Spiritual Self in Everyday Life: The Transformation of Personal Religious Experience in Nineteenth-Century New England*), gave me intellectual and artistic opportunities that public history could not provide. I could attach my argument to other academic studies of theology and religious history, as well as recent work in psychology, literary history, and political culture. I anchored my interpretations in the work of phenomenologist Alfred Schutz, anthropologist Mary Douglass, literary theorist Kenneth Burke, and sociologist Erving Goffman—none of them household names. My goal was simple. I hoped that this multidisciplinary approach would enrich the study of American religion in subsequent scholarly work. Perhaps in some small way in the years since it has. I may have been a noontime museologist. But at midnight I was locked onto my scholarly desk.

I could occasionally present museum visitors with snippets of this research, but it was plainly impossible to engage them in the full-blown taxonomy of conversion narratives that I developed for the dissertation—not in the brief moments of a visit to the Village Meetinghouse at OSV. But this doesn't mean that the museum encounter with history is any less intellectually challenging for visitors. It's different. Visitors don't exit our exhibitions having acquired a working overview of theological history or lots of new facts. And if they do, that information is not likely to be retained. Something more fundamental happens. I still often meet people who claim to have been deeply moved by the 2005 *Slavery in New York* exhibition at the New-York Historical Society (N-YHS). "Until I saw that show," a white New Yorker tells me, "I thought there were no black people in New York until the twentieth century." A black visitor, by contrast, says that she is confounded that the vital contribution of African skill and labor to the building of colonial New York was *never* represented in the city's visual record. "Are we black people always invisible here?" she asks. In my experience, visits to museums and historic sites can have a deep and transformative effect, reorienting one's sense of historical time and place. I always ask newbies in the history business what impelled their professional commitment to studying and teaching the past. Some credit a teacher, a few say they binged on Laura Ingalls Wilder, but the greater number attribute their interest to "going to Gettysburg with my Dad," or "the time I saw that exhibition about Japanese internment," or "seeing how small the [replica] *Mayflower* was, when we went to Plymouth," or even (to my delight) "when my fifth-grade class went to this awesome education building at Sturbridge." "Have you ever been there?" one of them asked.

Museum visitors are diverse, and we are responsible professionals. So we feel an obligation to get the history right. Public history may, if anything, be more intellectually demanding than academic teaching and writing. To deploy sources of such variety one has (in good scholarly conscience) to engage many unfamiliar fields of study. In 2011, for example, when American History Workshop wanted to include a beautiful piece of Louis XV furniture in our exhibition *Revolution! The Atlantic World Reborn* at N-YHS, the request prompted extra investigation, since we suspected that its mahogany had been harvested by enslaved men in the French colony of Saint-Domingue. We phoned the curator of the Musée des Arts Décoratifs in Paris. "Where did the mahogany come from?" we inquired. "We have never thought about that," came the wooden reply. For that exhibition alone, I also needed to develop a working knowledge of the history of British cartography, sugar-refining technology, French engravings of Napoleon and Toussaint, and the practice of vodou, among many other subjects. If I were writing about all of these, I could have more conveniently referred my readers to the work of other scholars. Unlike my academic peers, I couldn't make a living focusing on the nineteenth-century New Englanders whom I studied in my dissertation. They've had to share my investigative imagination with a wildly diverse brood—salmon cannery workers in Puget Sound, Gospel preachers in the Mississippi

Delta, railroad engineers in the Upper Midwest, enslaved African Americans in the Chesapeake, and working-class immigrants on New York's Lower East Side.

Furthermore, public historians have to learn a lot more about their audiences. Or at least they can't take advantage of the filters by which academic writing selects its reading public. Articles in academic journals are obviously most often addressed to specialist readers. Their opening paragraphs invariably flash a yellow sign to readers, even educated generalists, that the road ahead may be tricky for novices in the field. All scholars depend on the previously acquired knowledge of their publics. Young ones, in particular, aim to stress the cutting-edge nature of their contributions.

Pedagogically sensible public historians, instead, begin by surveying the current state of "common knowledge" in the fields they are interpreting. They know that they have to build upon what visitors and viewers bring to the history. To that they will have to add new evidence. Often such common historical knowledge is frozen into iconic word-pictures. "Slavery" is locked in an image of antebellum cotton plantations; "immigration," in teeming shiploads disembarking at Ellis Island; "industrial labor," in shirtless men at steel furnaces; "farmers," in figures behind horse-drawn plows. Many public history programs have to begin by explaining that each of these past institutions and practices has a more complex history and geography, a richer literature and anthropology. Half of my work as a historian, it often seems, is telling my visitors that what they thought was always true was actually rather evanescent and that what they thought was subject to frequent change was in fact consistently true.

Where the audience in academic arenas is fairly predictable, that for public history programs is highly diverse and variable. Museum attendance and public television viewership can be enormously expanded with marketing and promotion. Such efforts, well coordinated with the substance of the program itself, begin a process of bringing the uninitiated layperson into a more productive dialogue with the program. But perhaps equally important is the cultivation of specific audiences. Working with Haitian American churches and lodges, including programs on their own home turf, helped build a strong constituency for our *Revolution* exhibition at N-YHS. And cultivation goes beyond attracting attendees or viewers. Adapting public programs for in-school and youth audiences means understanding what issues and methods best motivate learning and engagement for each targeted group's developmental capacities and needs. Some years ago, we enlisted the help of a child psychologist and a master teacher to create three distinct interactive programs that used the same package of historical resources on New Amsterdam in 1660. The one for fifth-graders focused on a child's role in helping a family survive the frigid winter, eighth-graders explored the justice available to Africans accused of crime in the colony, and eleventh-grade students were challenged to maximize the profits of a voyage between the colony and the Dutch homeland. In a very real sense, I was applying what I had first learned about collaborating with the visitor/learner as a Sturbridge schoolmaster forty-odd years ago.

By contrast, in the scholarly writing that I do or that I read, or in my appearances as a university teacher, issues of audience are less urgent. It is more important, instead, to emphasize the widest and most globally significant contexts and connections for my evidence. That is how I prove myself a member of the community of professional historians. In my current research project, for example, I want to show how the acculturation of American immigrants was deeply affected by economic depression and war in the 1930s and 1940s, leading to particular pressures on family life, depending on ethnic characteristics, and shaping the fortunes of even the third and fourth generation in the late twentieth century. Note how my narrative framework employs terms derived from the social sciences—*acculturation, immigration, economic influences*, and so on. Further, as I plan my narrative I continue to propose transnational comparisons—what was it like for immigrants to France or South Africa during this same period? And comparisons to contemporary situations—do we see the same multigenerational issues arising in the wake of recent refugee crises?

Context, context, ever-widening contexts and critical comparisons. These are what, in my mind, set historical writing and teaching apart from mere antiquarian fact-mongering. They are, also, where I establish my allegiance to or dissent from the normal paradigms of scholarship in my field. Over the past generation, for instance, historians of slavery in the Old South have steadily widened the explanatory rhetoric of their arguments, as well as the scale and significance of the phenomena they study. Before the 1950s, it was common (except among African American and left-leaning scholars) to portray slavery as a paternalistic stewardship of mostly contented black people. Then there was an emphasis on the historical evolution and geographical differentiation of slave regimes. Today, antebellum slavery in the United States is increasingly viewed as an engine and expression of the expanding capitalist conquest and exploitation of non-white peoples in the wider Atlantic world (and also in the world of the Indian Ocean). Slowly, gently, our interpretations de-center the United States in the global history of slavery and the slave trade, infusing our narratives with Portuguese names and African places.

To summarize, academic work in history is best—at least in my mind—when it underscores the consequentiality of the issues it studies, when it helps explain the deep root-system of the actual forest of trees we encounter in looking at the past. To what extent, it asks, is this an economic, political, or cultural question, a source of contention between groups or a characteristic of the entire society? How is it different from what came before or what ensued afterwards? Public history is superior at the concrete and the particular, helping us see what sort of axe or saw-blade is best for cutting each species of tree in the woods. To shift the metaphor, public historians are teaching pros. They train fellow citizens in seeing the ball, in readying the stance and the racket, in following through. They aim to minimize the difference between their swing and yours.

There are, indeed, scholars who love the concrete and write brilliant evocations of precise places and moments in time. I always insist that newly arrived New Yorkers immediately read Robert G. Albion's delectable second chapter of *The Rise of New York Port* (1939). But, in all candor, I find that much recent academic writing reeks of the archive, suggesting that the scholar never trod the same soil with his or her subjects, or felt the same wind, or heard these words spoken aloud. I play a little game, tracing the scholar's movements from one source to another, as if the writing was about the relationship of one text to another, and not about the lives of real human beings. This tendency has drawn strength from the postmodern turn toward a focus on representation. We don't care much now about how old-time loggers cut down trees, now that we've discovered that the word *forest* is itself a contested cultural construct among historians.

In a parallel way, public historians adopt the context-broadening impulse of academic writing at their peril. A recent study of National Park Service interpretation in Lowell, Massachusetts, recommends that rangers tie their descriptions of work and living conditions in the mid-nineteenth-century New England mills to the contemporary struggles for fair treatment among textile workers in Bangladesh or Malaysia. Tempting as it to editorialize thus, it is dangerous to talk at length about what cannot actually be witnessed by site visitors. Sunday-afternoon leisure-time visitors are seldom seeking instruction about the modern world from interpreters, especially people younger than they, who may or may not be better informed than those visitors. Most tourists, in any case, do know a lot about the world today and can make these connections for themselves with only the merest hints of the historical parallel. When the visitors ask such questions or proffer their opinions, then it is more appropriate for the interpreter to provide some information to complicate that parallel.

We have to be wary of a widening gulf between the academic historian and the public historian. The future promises to divide them even further, to the detriment of both. Better support for graduate study and post-graduate research has, ironically, produced a generation of scholars who can reach their mid-thirties without ever having to consider audiences beyond other specialists and methods of reaching them. There are, of course, great exceptions to this—young scholars who have spent years teaching in K–12 schools and others who avidly embrace new pedagogies and instructional media. Still, I meet many scholars who have remained within the academic bubble since their pre-school years. They tell me how awkward they feel in the company of laypersons, except when they can discourse about their own particular research projects. And while they complain at length about academic administration, they seldom understand how their own vocation is implicated in the persistence and widening of class privilege and the ghettoization of intellectual labor in the university. The proliferation of dozens of public history courses and programs has, paradoxically, let many academic historians off the hook.

Meanwhile, their peers in the public world—hungry for ever-larger markets—are increasingly tempted to flatter their publics by sacrificing more complex and challenging interpretations of the past. They cherish what's called "user-generated content," which threatens to transform the museum into a festival marketplace of self-absorption. How can visitors generate content about periods in history so remote from their own, and how can they intuit and evaluate unfamiliar ways of interpreting human behavior? Anyone who has thrilled to a costume drama like *Wolf Hall* or *Hamilton* knows that compelling presentations of past cultures and historical moments do not overwhelm or paralyze visitors' engagement with the past. Successful teaching always acknowledges the learners' cognitive tools without discouraging curiosity about the unknown.

Both the overspecialized academic and the solipsistic educator underestimate the public's passion to explore the unfamiliar, which has been the fundamental characteristic of historical inquiry from the time of Herodotus forward. The public and the academic historian need each other to do what they do best, to complement (and also to compliment) one another. None of us knows where things will lead, but we are indebted to all historians who can tell us, physically and metaphorically, what track we follow, what milestones we passed, and what was our starting point for this journey together.

Paul J. Erickson
History and the Future of the Digital Humanities

OVER THE PAST decade, there have been countless conference panels, keynote addresses, and journal articles on the "future of history in the digital age." This essay is not going to address that question. It presumes that history has a future; there will be no mass disappearance of history departments. It also presumes that the digital age has been around for quite some time now, and thus a discussion of some epochal shift would be anachronistic. As is often the case with historians, there is debate over when the "Digital Age" started, and whether that is even the right name, but independent computer-to-computer networking began in 1969; Motorola launched the mobile phone in 1973; the first personal computers appeared in the late 1970s; and the World Wide Web was born in 1989. Those decades have not witnessed a decline in the vitality of the field of American history; rather, they have seen the field branch out in new directions, expanding our knowledge of the history of gender, race, sexuality, the Borderlands, the Atlantic World, and many other subfields. The origins of what used to be called "humanities computing" go back as far as 1949,

Paul J. Erickson is the Program Director for Arts, Humanities, and Culture and American Institutions, Society, and the Public Good at the American Academy of Arts and Sciences. Prior to joining the Academy, he worked for nine years as the Director of Academic Programs at the American Antiquarian Society in Worcester, Massachusetts. He holds a PhD from the Department of American Studies at the University of Texas at Austin.

when an Italian Jesuit scholar named Roberto Busa used punched cards to create a concordance to the writings of St. Thomas Aquinas, providing a useful origin myth for the digital humanities.[1] Indeed, as Julia Flanders notes, it has been decades since historians stopped viewing computers as "a specialized tool" and came to recognize them as "part of the tissue of the world."[2]

The advent of searchable databases of historical materials and the increasing ability of scholars to present their work through a range of innovative online platforms have changed the ambitions of individual scholars, the expectations of their employers, and the desires of their readers. This essay will discuss some of the effects of these changes, as well as some things that might be done to help historians address those changes more effectively. While this volume is titled "The Future of History," I would argue that there is no such thing as "History" in this sense. The past exists, of course, as does the discipline that includes scholars who study and interpret it. But there is no single entity that we can point to and say, "That's History." Discussing "history" as a unitary thing that may or may not have a future is impossible. Rather, history in this sense is made up of professional societies of historians; history departments at colleges and universities; and the institutions (such as libraries, archives, and museums) that collect, preserve, and make available the objects and texts that historians study. So in addressing the role of the digital humanities in the future of the field of American history, I will address how some of the sets of institutions that make up what we think of as the "discipline" can engage with scholars and their audiences to take advantage of the possibilities offered by new digital approaches to research, writing, and publication.

Defining what "digital humanities" is (or is not) is a cottage industry in the field, and its flexibility and lack of boundaries are two of the field's most attractive features for many practitioners (I use the term "field" here with some caution, as there is still significant debate over whether "digital humanities" is a field, a method, an approach, a genre, a medium, or a shared set of concerns). While many scholars have pointed to qualities that are often found in digital humanities projects—interdisciplinarity, collaboration, de-centering of authorship, dependence on infrastructure—these are not necessarily unique to the digital humanities. The *Digital Humanities Manifesto* 2.0 (2009) defines the digital humanities as "not a unified field but *an array of convergent practices* that explore a universe in which: a) print is no longer the exclusive or the normative medium in which knowledge is produced and/or disseminated; instead, print finds itself absorbed into new, multimedia configurations; and b) digital tools, techniques, and media have altered the production and dissemination of knowledge in the arts, human and social sciences."[3] This definition serves to describe the fundamental tenets of the approach. On a more practical level, the digital humanities for the purposes of this essay can be understood to encompass the use of computational methods (beyond word processing) for conducting research or presenting findings that could not be done any other way, the presentation of old media forms on digital platforms (remediation) with the addition of metadata that add meaning to or information about the original media form, the use of technology to reshape the humanities classroom, and the transformation of scholarly communication and readers' interaction with scholarship through the presentation of work on digital platforms.

When many people in the academy write about the "digital humanities," they are actually referring to its manifestation in literary studies. Digital humanities approaches found their first and most congenial homes in English departments because the power of new information technologies was most readily applied to bodies of text, and thus these approaches became incorporated into textual study.[4] But over the past decades historians have also been active in the field, and "digital history" has developed some characteristics that distinguish it from work done in other disciplines, most notably (according to Stephen Robertson) in its long-standing emphasis on using digital materials in teaching and in its use of computational tools.[5] Digital history scholarship concerns itself with examining and representing the past; it uses new information technologies to create frameworks that allow people to experience, read, and annotate an argument about the past. Unlike traditional modes of scholarship, digital history enables readers to form their own interpretive associations, since information is usually not presented in a linear style typical of a museum exhibition, journal article, or monograph. Digital history makes use of sources in digital form to produce works of digital scholarship that present readers with, in Will Thomas's words, a "suite of interpretive elements, ways to gain leverage on the problem under investigation."[6] This de-centering of the author, and the concomitant surrender of some portion of interpretive control from author to reader, is one of the most salient features of presenting any form of scholarship in a digital format.

New technologies have given historians the ability to search much larger bodies of digitized texts, not simply for keywords but also in more sophisticated ways including text mining and topic modeling.[7] Digital tools have also enabled historians to manipulate source materials in new ways: extracting geographic data from texts in order to create maps, overlaying historical photographs to assess changes in the landscape and built environment, and using virtual reality software to recreate historic spaces. In addition to the different interpretive model inherent in most works of digital history scholarship, another critical difference between digital and analog historical scholarship is that digital projects are open to continual revision, as technologies shift and engagements with new historiographies emerge.

Change, then, is perhaps the most salient quality of digital history, and of the digital humanities more broadly. Compared to the relative stability of print forms (even as there have been tremendous structural changes in the world of academic publishing), the forms that digital humanities projects have taken have transformed enormously in the span of only a few years. To take only one example of the type of platform change that is characteristic of digital history projects, the Trans-Atlantic Slave Trade Database has morphed from multiple machine-readable datasets produced in the 1970s and '80s to a CD-ROM issued in 1999 to a publicly accessible web-based database launched in 2008 that has had new features and data added consistently ever since. Many of the most frequently cited articles on the practice of digital history were written before the social media revolution transformed the ways that people interact and find information online. And it is still unclear whether digital history's future lies in assimilating familiar modes of scholarship into digital domains or in developing entirely new methodologies and research questions that eventually come to constitute a distinct discipline. Thus, it is always risky to offer any statements on what digital history ought to look like, since the only thing we know for sure is that it will look different in five years. The experimentation that makes this level of change possible is part of what makes the digital humanities an exciting field, but it does not always mesh easily with the institutional imperatives of life in the humanities. How does a field that emphasizes interdisciplinary and cross-institutional collaboration using open-source data and tools enable scholars to claim "ownership" of their work in ways that are legible to funders, presses, libraries, and university administrations? And how can the institutions that make up the discipline of history adjust their practices to encourage the level of experimentation that the field of digital history needs, instead of attempting to impose a professionally sanctioned form of digital scholarship? In the remainder of this essay, I will offer some suggestions for each of the various institutional types that make up the discipline (as well as for individual scholars) that can help increase the likelihood that digital history will be embraced as an opportunity rather than being viewed as a challenge.

DISCIPLINARY AND PROFESSIONAL ORGANIZATIONS

In 2008, the National Endowment for the Humanities' Digital Humanities Initiative became the Office of Digital Humanities, which meant that the program had a permanent place within the agency's structure (and a secure budget line). And even before that date other major funders in the humanities—including the Andrew W. Mellon Foundation and the American Council of Learned Societies—were offering support for projects in the digital humanities. There are numerous successful digital history projects that owe their current status to start-up grants from the NEH or ACLS. But what else can disciplinary and professional organizations do to ensure that the discipline of history will benefit from the advances embodied in the digital humanities and to affirm digital history scholarship's place in the mainstream of the discipline?

First, continue to offer grant support for digital history projects. Projects in the digital humanities typically have higher start-up costs than traditional humanities projects, and many colleges and universities cannot support these costs alone (or are reluctant to do so when the collaborators on a project come from multiple institutions). It is both simplistic and repetitive to say that funding matters, but: Funding matters.

Second, recognize excellence in digital history. The National Council on Public History each year presents the Outstanding Public History Award to a project that "contributes to a broader public reflection and appreciation of the past or that serves as a model of professional public history practice." Several digital history projects have received this one thousand dollar prize since its inception in 2008. Since 2009, the American Historical Association and the Roy Rosenzweig Center for History and New Media at George Mason University have awarded the Roy Rosenzweig Prize for Innovation in Digital History to an "innovative and freely available new media project, and in particular for work that reflects thoughtful, critical, and rigorous engagement with technology and the practice of history." The four thousand dollar prize is only open to projects launched within the previous two years, and it is intended to support further development of the project. In 2012, the AHA announced the *American Historical Review* Prize for the Best Digital Article.[8] Beyond these prizes, however, there are few recognition opportunities for works of digital history. And the prizes that continue to garner the most attention in the field of American history—the Bancroft Prize, the Pulitzer Prize, the National Book Award, the George Washington Book Prize, and the Frederick Douglass Book Prize—all are awarded to books (and include much larger sums of money), reinforcing the message that history remains a book discipline. Until there is a Bancroft Prize for digital history—or until a digital project wins one of these major prizes—digital history projects will likely continue to be seen as a world apart.

As the AHA is the primary professional organization for historians, it sets a pattern that many organizations and departments follow. Its annual conferences have featured digital history projects in larger numbers and in more visible venues in recent years, and the meetings now welcome innovative presentation formats that are better suited to digital history projects than the traditional panel model. These trends should continue, and program committees for all history conferences should ensure that there are distinct time slots and presentation formats made available to scholars who wish to present digital projects.

A surprisingly small percentage of history positions ask for candidates with a primary or secondary specialization in digital humanities (only 12 percent in the 2015–2016 cycle, according to Rob Townsend and Emily Swafford). This request in job listings is likely to appear more frequently in the coming years and represents a trend that the AHA should take a more visible role in tracking.[9] The AHA's most significant step in addressing the discipline's future with respect to the digital humanities was the formal approval in June 2015 of *Guidelines for the Professional Evaluation of Digital Scholarship by Historians*. These guidelines, which followed the Modern Language Association's publication of their own set of evaluation standards in 2012, seem to operate from a stance of disciplinary suspicion towards the digital humanities, placing the onus on individual scholars to justify and explain their decision to pursue a digital project. Future guidelines from the AHA and other disciplinary organizations on the evaluation of digital projects will hopefully both more fully embrace digital history as an opportunity rather than an oddity and provide more specific guidelines for departments to use in evaluating digital projects.

DEPARTMENTS

Individual history departments are the institutional homes of most professional historians, and thus how they support, evaluate, and teach digital history will have the most significant impact on whether historians decide to pursue digital projects. Perhaps the most significant step that history departments can take is to clarify whether they consider digital projects as part of historical scholarship *per se*, or if they consider them to be "public history." Different departments teach public history classes and reward public history projects in different ways, so clarifying where the department sees digital projects fitting within the discipline is crucial to providing individual scholars with guidance about how they should pursue their digital projects. One would hope that departments would pay attention to the state of digital history *now* when they make these decisions, rather than referring back to a recollection of the early days of the field. While many digital history projects in the past fifteen years have been public history projects, it is clear that digital approaches are being used in more scholarly and interpretive ways and, therefore, should not be thought of only as tools for communicating to a broader audience.

Ideally, all history departments would be able to have faculty lines on the tenure track dedicated to digital history, and they would be able to provide IT and academic computing resources to digital historians (although these resources could well be shared across departments, which would reinforce a school's commitment to collaborative work). Given the budget constraints under which most history departments operate, however, these will be difficult goals to meet. Departments should make an effort to ensure that they have faculty resources to teach courses in digital history and that they have the technological resources to support student projects. They should also make an effort to ensure that they are not left with *only one* faculty member (often a junior member) who does digital scholarship, as that person would constantly be in the position of having to "explain" digital history to his or her colleagues.

For the purposes of tenure and promotion, the AHA guidelines provide a starting point, but individual departments need leaders who will establish guidelines for how digital projects will be evaluated, and departments then need to adhere to those guidelines. And it is important that these be standards *not* for what digital projects ought to look like but for how they will be evaluated (that is to say, rather than asking if something looks like other digital history projects, evaluators should determine if a project has succeeded in meeting goals that the project team set at the beginning of the work). Departmental guidelines for tenure and promotion must also clearly state how collaborative projects will be evaluated, especially those of an interdisciplinary and cross-institutional nature; how reward systems structured around "authorship" will function for projects that often do not have a single author; what standards will be used to assess the impact of a digital project (web analytics, reviews, citations, etc.); and whether a digital project must have a companion print component in order to count for tenure and promotion. Promotion committees that are asked to evaluate digital projects ought to contain at least one member who also primarily works in digital history.

LIBRARIES AND ARCHIVES

Libraries and archives are crucial to the digital humanities overall, and to digital history in particular. The digital humanities by definition relies on working with digitized versions of texts, and libraries and archives play a central role in digitizing historical materials and making them available to digital humanities scholars for use. Partnerships with libraries and librarians have been particularly crucial to digital historians, given that many of the earliest and most successful projects in the field were essentially digitization efforts.

Contrary to the often-expressed belief that "everything is already online," there are still vast amounts of undigitized material in libraries and archives in the United States. (I am speaking here primarily of independent research libraries and special collections libraries, like that of the Massachusetts Historical Society, not general research collections).[10] The most important contribution that these institutions can make to ensuring the future vitality of digital history is to digitize as many of those materials as possible, in high-quality scans with robust metadata attached, and make the files openly available through databases that have an API (application program interface) that enables scholars to access the complete data. This is a tall order, if not an impossible one, but it should be the goal. Many libraries have benefited from the digitization of their materials by for-profit vendors who sell subscriptions to proprietary databases. The materials in these databases are effectively invisible to people without academic affiliations or who work at institutions that cannot afford to subscribe. It is incumbent upon libraries that have digitized their materials in this way to make the full scans openly available as soon as is contractually possible. As Daniel Cohen noted in 2008, "Open access to historical scholarship is about human audiences; open access to primary sources is about machine audiences."[11] Historians simply cannot do sophisticated digital history scholarship without open access to full texts of historical documents. The digitization of manuscript materials poses many more challenges, since most of these materials still need to be transcribed before they can be of use to digital humanities scholars. Archives cannot be expected to do that work themselves, but they should erect as few obstacles as possible to the work of scholars who seek access to manuscript materials that they hope to use in their digital projects, either for public access or for their own data analysis.

Libraries and archives possess another enormous source of data that would be of use to digital humanities scholars: the metadata contained in their OPACs (online public access catalogs). These data are often invisible to search engines, so some scholars may not be fully aware of their research potential. Making both general and copy-specific catalog data available to scholars in machine-readable format is a valuable contribution to scholars working on digital projects, particularly in the field of book history.

Libraries and archives often operate under financial constraints even more stringent than those facing humanities departments, and adding staff is often impossible. But if these institutions are to capitalize on the opportunities that the digital revolution presents in terms of making their collections more broadly available, and if they wish to encourage digital projects, dedicating at least one full-time staff position to digital humanities work would be an important step. The position description should specify sophisticated technical skills as well as familiarity with the range of disciplinary approaches within the digital humanities. Along with a commitment to dedicated staff should come an investment in the technological infrastructure that enables scholars to work on digital projects while visiting a library and also that securely stores the institution's digitized materials. It is much easier to lose digital data than physical items, so the goal should be to hold the physical embodiments of the digital data (i.e., hard drives) on site, with copies of the data stored remotely.

Libraries that offer visiting research fellowships should make clear that scholars working on digital projects are welcome to apply on the same footing as scholars working on projects destined for print publication. These fellowships provide an important avenue of access both to collection materials and to curatorial expertise, and they also serve as visible forms of recognition within the discipline. These competitions should welcome proposals for digital projects, and reviewers of these applications should be capable of evaluating proposals for such projects on their own terms. Institutions may also wish to rethink some of the traditional parameters of the visiting research fellowship model (one to three consecutive months in residence, focused entirely on research). Many scholars working in digital history are not in tenure ladder positions (many work as public historians) and thus are not able to leave the demands of their jobs for an extended research fellowship, but they might be able to accept a fellowship of a shorter duration.

Given the complications of maintaining the hardware and software systems required to present digital projects in their original form, it is unrealistic to expect libraries to take on the extra responsibility of preserving the many digital scholarship projects that draw on their collections. But libraries should be part of the conversation about how (and if) digital history projects themselves ought to be preserved. Some creators of digital projects may not necessarily intend for the projects to be permanent, but those scholars who do want their digital scholarship to be preserved will likely have to take on that responsibility themselves.

INDIVIDUAL SCHOLARS

The focus of this essay has been on the institutions that combine to make up the discipline of history and on how they can adapt to fit the reality that historians have been doing digital history for more than a generation. In 2003, Roy Rosenzweig wondered if historians working in the digital realm would be confronted by scarcity or abundance: scarcity, because digital materials are so fragile, or abundance, because storage and networked computing combine to make it possible to save and make available vast quantities of data.[12] At this point, it is clear that the hard drives have won, and abundance is the challenge—historians face an archive of sources that is effectively infinite.

In such a world, a methodological approach rooted in close reading of a small number of texts seems anachronistic. Yet some historians will continue to choose to do such work and will generate new and exciting insights. The "future of history" is not that *every* scholar will choose to do digital projects, just as it will not be the case that *every* reader will only want to read history from a laptop or a mobile phone (or through a virtual reality headset). Just as in the past, individual scholars will have to make choices about the medium in which they want to present their scholarship, based on the sources they are working with, the argument they are trying to make, and the audience they are hoping to reach.

Much of the early excitement about digital approaches to the past was that they offered a chance to "democratize history." By presenting historical materials without the alienating apparatus of footnotes and citations to scholarship, the argument went, historians would be able to speak directly to non-specialist audiences. But there is nothing inherent in a digital mode of presentation that makes historical work more accessible, just as there is nothing inherent in the technology of print that automatically makes history distant or elitist.

As Tom Scheinfeldt has written, many digital history projects have tended to focus on developing tools or resources rather than on making arguments, but this is changing, and that shift will continue as the genre of digital history develops conventions and subgenres of its own.[13] In twenty-five years, these questions about the "future of history" will seem pointless, as digital work will simply be how people do history. But in the meantime, how should historians who may not be full-fledged digital humanities practitioners approach the world of digital history?

The easy answer, as in all things, is to do what feels right. If a project benefits from a digital component, investigate how to build one, and ask for help from colleagues who have experience. The questions that one asks—about argument and presentation of sources and audience—can be the same as for a work of print history. But how one goes about achieving those goals will be different.

Historians should free themselves from the notion that digital history is the same thing as public history. Digital approaches do indeed make it possible to reach a much larger public than traditional print scholarship reaches. And most public history projects at this point already include a digital component (although this should also not be a necessity). But even if a digital history project is not aspiring to do the work of public history, it still needs to accommodate the particular affordances of the form. Scholars working in digital modes need to resist the temptation to structure their digital projects like an article or a monograph, with an introduction, a set of sections that advance the argument (typically chronologically), and a conclusion. Given that most people discover digital history projects through a web search, very few readers enter a project at the home page and proceed through it in order. The shift to digital modes of presentation requires new skills of scholars (and new kinds of training for graduate students): the ability to write history that will engage general readers and the imagination to structure digital projects so that readers can enter a project at any point and navigate their way through without misconstruing the project's larger interpretive points. If the old challenge facing writers of historical scholarship was *discoverability* (How will people find what we write?), the new problem will be *stickiness* (How do we get people to stay with a project once they've found it?).

Aside from identifying an audience and then writing to reach that audience, historians also have to modify some traditional habits of the discipline in order to flourish professionally in the digital world. In a landscape where university presses are less central to the publishing enterprise, individual scholars will have greater responsibility for ensuring that their scholarship is available and visible online (and that it meets the same standards of accuracy as print scholarship). They should make every effort to ensure that their scholarship appears in open access publications instead of behind paywalls, which is a near-guarantee of invisibility. And as the world of digital history takes shape, individual scholars should also work to develop new forms of peer review that are suited to evaluating projects with collective authorship. Recognizing the many contributors—technologists, archivists, designers, writers—to digital history projects in ways that benefit all of their careers is essential, as is insisting on systems of professional advancement that integrate these changes into how history scholarship is produced.

HISTORIAN Cameron Blevins has noted that, for almost fifteen years, discussions of digital history have been couched in the future tense, with the terms *promise*, *possibilities*, and *potential* being consistent presences in the titles of papers, panels, and articles about the field.[14] While any field of digital scholarship is by definition oriented towards what new tools and technologies are just over the horizon, at this point we can say, enough. Digital history is here. While digital methods of doing research and presenting scholarship will change over time and will continue to reshape the field, it is time to acknowledge that at least part of the future of history will be digital. The institutions that make up the discipline of history—professional associations, departments, and libraries and archives—still have work to do to ensure that digital historical scholarship is produced professionally, evaluated rigorously, and evaluated equitably. But to continue to speak of digital history as that which is yet to come is to ignore what is happening today. The future of history is now.

1 For the most detailed history of this origin story of humanities computing, see Steven E. Jones, *Roberto Busa, S.J., and the Emergence of Humanities Computing: The Priest and the Punched Cards* (New York, 2016). For an excellent summary of the more recent shifts in the field of digital history, see Cameron Blevins, "Digital History's Perpetual Future Tense," in *Debates in the Digital Humanities 2016*, ed. Lauren F. Klein and Matthew K. Gold (Minneapolis, 2016), available at http://dhdebates .gc.cuny.edu/debates/text/77.

2 Julia Flanders, "The Productive Unease of 21st-Century Digital Scholarship," *Digital Humanities Quarterly* 3, no. 3 (2009), available at http://digitalhumanities.org /dhq/vol/3/3/000055/000055.html.

3 The collectively authored text of the *Digital Humanities Manifesto* 2.0 is available at http://manifesto.humanities.ucla.edu/2009/05/29/the-digital-humanities-manifesto-20/.

4 For a cogent explanation of why this is the case, see Matthew Kirschenbaum, "What Is Digital Humanities and What Is It Doing in English Departments?," in *Debates in the Digital Humanities*, ed. Matthew K. Gold (Minneapolis, 2012). See also Amy E. Earhart, *Traces of the Old, Uses of the New: The Emergence of the Digital Literary Studies* (Ann Arbor, 2015).

5 Stephen Robertson, "The Differences between Digital Humanities and Digital History," in *Debates in the Digital Humanities 2016*, available at http://dhdebates.gc.cuny.edu/debates/text/76.

6 Daniel J. Cohen, Michael Frisch, Patrick Gallagher, Steven Mintz, Kirsten Sword, Amy Murrell Taylor, William G. Thomas III, and William J. Turkel, "Interchange: The Promise of Digital History," *Journal of American History* 95(2008):454.

7 Text mining, a subset of data mining, is the process of analyzing large bodies of written text in order to generate *new* forms of information, typically through the use of specialized software that can suggest connections, categorize information, make links between otherwise unconnected documents, and create visual maps of the text corpus being studied. Topic modeling refers to the analysis of a text (or group of texts) to look for patterns in the use of words and phrases. To the software that is being used, a "topic" is simply a word or set of words that occurs in statistically meaningful ways. By helping reveal the hidden semantic structures of a set of texts, topic modeling can help organize large bodies of unstructured text (e.g., a run of Boston newspapers from 1765 to 1787).

8 The application instructions for this prize provide by far the most explicit (and some would say limiting) set of guidelines for what qualifies an article as a work of *digital* history that I have seen, and are worth examining. See the call for submissions in *Perspectives on History: The Newsmagazine of the American Historical Association*, Feb. 2012, at the AHA website: www.historians.org.

9 Robert B. Townsend and Emily Swafford, "Conflicting Signals in the Academic Job Market for History," *Perspectives on History*, Jan. 2017.

10 While it is hardly a fail-safe distinction, I am using *libraries* to refer to collections primarily made up of printed material and *archives* to refer to collections of primarily manuscript materials. Many institutions hold both types of materials, of course, but from the standpoint of digitization, which relies on optical character recognition software, the distinction here is meaningful, even if it is not quite so clear-cut in practice. See Paul Erickson, "Where the Evidence Is: or, Willie Sutton Visits the Library," *J19: The Journal of Nineteenth-Century Americanists* 2(2014):186-194.

11 Daniel J. Cohen, "Interchange: The Promise of Digital History," *Journal of American History* 95(2008):474.

12 Roy Rosenzweig, "Scarcity or Abundance? Preserving the Past in a Digital Era," *American Historical Review* 108(2003):735-762.

13 Tom Scheinfeldt, "Where's the Beef? Does Digital Humanities Have to Answer Questions?," in *Debates in the Digital Humanities*, available at http://dhdebates .gc.cuny.edu/debates/text/18.

14 Blevins, "Digital History's Perpetual Future Tense."

Louise Mirrer What Does History Cost and How Can We Pay for It?

WHAT DOES IT COST *NOT* TO DO HISTORY?

A lot has changed since I somewhat impertinently revised the top-ic I'd been asked to address at the Massachusetts Historical Society workshop on the future of history, from "What does history cost?" to "What is the cost of not doing history?"

I was, at the time of the program, emboldened to make my revi-sion after reading an article written by historian Niall Ferguson, one of my institution's trustees, together with historian Graham Allison. The piece, entitled "Why the President Needs a Council of Historians," gave dramatic evidence of the heavy cost—including in human lives—that results when history, and/or the advice of historians, is uninvited or ignored.[1]

Allison and Ferguson's article presented several compelling exam-ples, among them one that was striking for its suggestion that historical

Louise Mirrer is President and CEO of the New-York Historical Society. Under her leadership, N-YHS has become a center for public engagement in, and enjoyment of, history and art, with a half million visitors annually onsite and several million visitors online. Dr. Mirrer has led her institution in two major capital campaigns, raising a total of $135 million. In her previous role as Executive Vice Chancellor and Provost for the City University of New York system, she spearheaded a hiring initiative in American history at CUNY's undergraduate colleges and introduced American history as a requirement for CUNY undergraduates. She holds master's and doctoral degrees from Stanford University and a Diploma in Linguistics from Cambridge University. She is an honorary fellow of Wolfson College, Cambridge.

knowledge could have changed the course of American involvement in Iraq:

> In 2003, . . . when President George W. Bush chose to topple Saddam Hussein, he did not appear to fully appreciate either the difference between Sunni and Shiite Muslims or the significance of the fact that Saddam's regime was led by a Sunni minority that had suppressed the Shiite majority. He failed to heed warnings that the predictable consequence of his actions would be a Shiite-dominated Baghdad beholden to the Shiite champion in the Middle East—Iran.

Another example offered in the article underscored the benefits of relying on leaders who are knowledgeable about history, especially when those leaders' knowledge directly relates to their jobs. Ben Bernanke, a student of history and, particularly, of earlier financial crises, served as chairman of the Federal Reserve following the 2008 financial meltdown. "Bernanke's Fed," Allison and Ferguson write,

> acted decisively, using unprecedented tools that stretched—if not exceeded—the Fed's legal powers, such as buying up mortgage-backed and Treasury securities in what was called quantitative easing. Bernanke's knowledge of the Depression also informed the Fed's efforts to backstop other central banks.

In his memoirs, Bernanke called the context of history "invaluable" to his decision making. Judging from the nodding-in-assent heads of workshop participants when I cited Bernanke's characterization of history's worth, the significant expenditures at some history-themed institutions—including my own—which we went on to discuss, seemed well worthwhile. The cost of *not* doing history was just too high.

Today, less than one year after the workshop, history, it would seem, could not be more actively, or avidly, pursued. In a sharply divided nation, both sides emphatically ground their views in the American past, one side using history to advocate a return to a time when the United States was different from how it is today—more homogeneous and more isolated from the rest of the world—the other using history to stress America's founding ideas of freedom and equality, rejecting curbs on civil rights and immigration based on ethnic origins or religious tests.

Still, I would argue, the cost of *not* doing history remains intolerably high. What we are seeing today, and often on both sides, is not "doing history" but "cherry-picking" history—a failure, in my view, to give credence to the consensual decrees that have resulted, over the course of American history, in American policies and laws.

WHAT DOES HISTORY COST?

History, according to the data we looked at and discussed during the program session, can cost quite a lot. Using the New-York Historical Society as an example shows that a medium-sized institution might spend between $25 and $30 million annually to support a mix of rotating and permanent exhibitions, education, public programs, and scholarly research. Capital projects have to be layered over annual operating costs, so that, for example, in the case of New-York Historical,

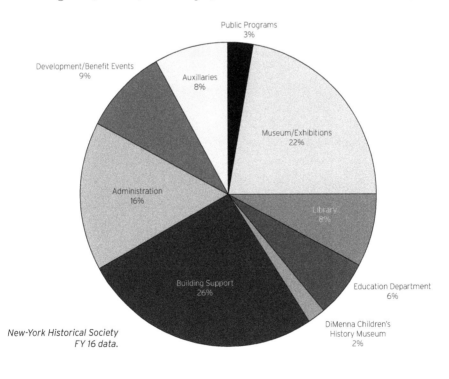

Public Programs
3%

Development/Benefit Events
9%

Auxillaries
8%

Museum/Exhibitions
22%

Administration
16%

Library
8%

Building Support
26%

Education Department
6%

DiMenna Children's
History Museum
2%

*New-York Historical Society
FY 16 data.*

over the past dozen years an additional $150 million has been spent on renovations as well as routine building repairs.

History costs even more at larger institutions. Construction and exhibition installations alone at the recently opened National Museum of African American History and Culture (NMAAHC) on the National Mall in Washington, D.C., cost $540 million.

There are many reasons for the sometimes enormous cost of history, especially today. Visitors to history-themed institutions tend to expect state-of-the-art, technologically enhanced permanent and rotating shows as well as expensive amenities such as destination restaurants, multi-media experiences, and immersive films.

State and local governments may also have an impact on history's cost, with expectations and/or needs like participation in helping to educate children in a state or city's public schools. At the New-York Historical Society, for example, where public school partnerships are a priority, 40 educators serve some 200,000 New York City public school students at an annual cost of nearly $2 million.

Rotating exhibitions have been called the "heroin" of twenty-first-century museums. These exhibitions can cost a lot. Drawing on two recent, temporary shows at New-York Historical, *WWII & NYC* and *Chinese American: Exclusion/Inclusion*, establishes a typical cost of nearly $3 million apiece.

But history-themed institutions can ill afford to ignore survey data that show that visitors are more likely to plan their visits around a special exhibition than a permanent installation. In surveys over the past five years, New-York Historical has found that a full 71 percent of visitors tie their visit to a specific, temporary show. Only 5 percent of visitors said that they came to New-York Historical specifically to see permanent collections.

There are myriad other costs associated with doing history at museums and historic homes and sites, among them storage for priceless collections of books, documents, manuscripts, ephemera, and art. The chart on the facing page shows the rising cost over the past five years at New-York Historical for offsite storage, necessary to house a vast and growing collection.

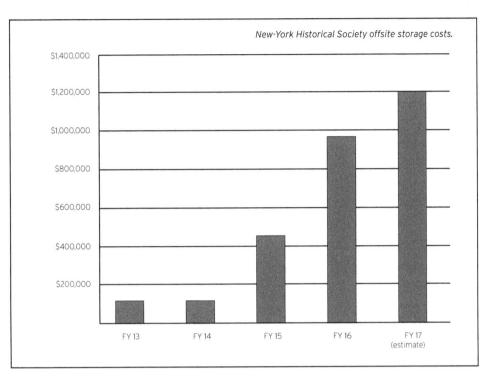

New-York Historical Society offsite storage costs.

FY 13	FY 14	FY 15	FY 16	FY 17 (estimate)

HOW DO WE PAY FOR HISTORY?

To pay the costs of history, history-themed institutions typically rely on a mix of funding streams: earned income (including admission fees, memberships, gift sales, and space rentals), grants, donations, and endowment draws. Most institutions look to both public and private sources for funding. As might be expected, substantial public dollars support our national history museums.

Though federal agencies such as the National Endowment for the Humanities and the Institute for Museum and Library Services support a range of humanities endeavors, these kinds of public funds are critical to the lifeblood of many history museums, enabling special education and programmatic initiatives with significant, though not predictable, grants in the thousands to tens and hundreds of thousands and even million dollar range. A scan of 2016 NEH grants shows support for a wide variety of geographically disparate history-themed institutions, ranging from the Fullerton Museum Center in California, to the Colorado Historical Society in Denver, to the State Historical Society of Iowa in Des Moines, to the Newberry Library in Chicago, to West Florida Historic Preservation, Inc., in Pensacola, to the Brooklyn Historical Society in New York City.

Funding of selected federal agencies that support humanities activities (constant 2016 dollars, in millions):[2]

	FY08	FY15	FY16 Request
NEH	162.04	147.81	147.94
NPS Heritage Partnership	17.10	20.57	9.95
NPS Historic Preservation	78.82	57.10	89.91
NPS Remainder of Budget	3,033.19	2,569.13	2,947.85
IMLS Library Services	226.12	184.96	188.35
IMLS Museum Services	35.02	30.50	35.08
NARA NHPRC	10.64	5.06	5.00
NARA remainder of budget	449.72	381.34	384.07
Smithsonian NMAAHC	5.20	41.15	41.50
Smithsonian NMAH	24.18	22.03	23.12
Smithsonian NMAI	35.36	31.83	32.08
LoC	434.99	418.07	438.02

State and local governments can also be major players in paying history's costs. New York City institutions officially "owned" by the city, like the Museum of the City of New York (not New-York Historical, which is private), receive approximately 10 percent of their operating budget from public funds. And private donors have become increasingly critical to paying costs at history museums and like organizations. "Patriotic philanthropist" David Rubenstein, for example, has made multi-million dollar gifts to institutions including the Thomas Jefferson Foundation, Montpelier, Mount Vernon, the National Archives, the Sewell-Belmont House and Museum, and the NMAAHC. Richard Gilder and Robert H. Smith are other examples of private donors associated with millions of dollars in support for history.

Though much corporate funding has dried up over the past decade, companies like American Express and Mars continue to dedicate significant resources to American "heritage" preservation efforts. Foundations also provide significant support for history. Among the larger ones are the Rockefeller Foundation, the Andrew W. Mellon Foundation, and the Ford Foundation.

ACADEMIC INSTITUTIONS

As both the data and the discussion during our session confirmed, the cost of, and payment for, history at American academic institutions has taken a somewhat different path. Though the sources of revenue at academic institutions may be similar to those at history museums and historic homes and sites, declining public support for public colleges and universities has surely taken a toll. History is one of several disciplines in which expenditures have sharply decreased.

An American Academy of Arts and Sciences (AAAS) Lincoln Project report notes that public research universities have seen an average 26 percent decrease since 2008: "For the first time in the history of American public higher education, tuition has become the principal revenue source for many public research universities."[3] To cope with the decline in public funding, public institutions of higher education have revised their business models, using a combination of government mandates and priorities and student enrollment in majors to guide the distribution of funds. Institutions have also favored funding for STEM subjects over humanities disciplines like history, based on the assumption that graduates in these fields will earn more money and contribute more to the public good. All of these trends have affected staffing in history departments, where there has been a decline in the number of majors and where faculty are becoming fewer and more junior, with part-time and adjunct positions on the rise.

Organization of American Historians Pres. Nancy F. Cott lamented the situation at public academic institutions, commenting that,

> The decline in the number of history majors . . . stems from more than students' supposed "practicality" in choosing majors that seem

to lead more directly to career earnings. States are weighing in. State funding not only literally produces what courses will be offered and credited, but also—insofar as the public is aware of state priorities—state action affects how individuals think about their conduct of life and their choices. This is an additional way that money talks.[4]

Academic participants in our session agreed with President Cott, many opining, with a palpable sense of despair, that future prospects for meaningful financial support for history from academic institutions— private as well as public—were dim. Still the academic historians, as well the institutional leaders in the room, saw a glimmer of hope in the growing link between academic history and history museums. Not only has there been an increase in interest in the field of public history, with American history PhDs in demand for museum jobs and foundations such as Mellon supporting public history fellowships for history pre- and post-docs, but many history-themed institutions have come to rely on academic historians to attract donor support for public programs as part of their missions around public engagement.

AT THE TIME of the workshop, presidential election campaign rhetoric already was suggestive of an orientation toward the past. Remarks by candidate Donald J. Trump, for example, relied heavily on slogans like "Make America Great Again"—presumably referring to a time or times in history when America was greater than it is today—and "America First," the name of a World War II–era antiwar group whose vision, at least as articulated by its spokesperson, Charles Lindbergh, was that Western nations "can have peace and security only so long as we band together to preserve that most priceless possession, our inheritance of European blood."[5]

Although our discussion did, from time to time, invoke the campaign, none of us took such references to history as evidence that we were about to enter a period in which historical knowledge would have an impact on policy. Indeed, many of us expressed agreement with Allison and Ferguson's assessment of American policy makers, as articulated in this quip: "It is sometimes said that most Americans live in 'the United States of Amnesia.' Less widely recognized is how many American policy makers live there too."

But today there are policy makers in the White House and advisors to the president who base their proposals for policy interventions on precedents and historical analogues about which they are well informed—even though historians and others may disagree with their views of the past. President Trump's first executive order banning travel from seven majority-Muslim nations, for example, was defended by some of these policy makers and advisors in vividly historical terms, with a century and a half of data to show how immigration in America has been restricted as much as, or even more than, it has been allowed to freely flow.

Historians and organizations representing historians have seen things differently, advocating the importance of historical thinking, urging policy makers to consult the historical record, persuaded that such consultation will, in the end, lead to an understanding of, for example, the harmful impact of restrictive policies that have intentionally excluded specific groups—as well as the benefits that America has reaped thanks to its varied cultures, races, religions, and ethnicities.

But such sharp divisions only reinforce the point that the work of our institutions is well worth the cost. We need to know and understand the past in order to engage in these debates. Above all, we need to educate people so that they appreciate that American history has always been about debate, from the full year leading up to the ratification of our Constitution 230 years ago, when Americans were invited to participate in discussions about how our nation should be.

Building on the workshop theme of the future of history, I want to suggest, in conclusion, that as we formulate our budgets and proceed to spend, we look ahead as well as back. What will and what should America be like 230 years from now?

1 Graham Allison and Niall Ferguson, "Why the U.S. President Needs a Council of Historians," *Atlantic*, Sept. 2016.

2 This data is drawn from the American Academy of Arts and Sciences, Humanities Indicators, "National Endowment for the Humanities (NEH) Funding Levels," as

presented October 2015, Table IV-2: Federal Support of Humanities Activities, Fiscal Years 2008–2016 (Adjusted for Inflation). Current figures available at www .humanitiesindicators.org/content/indicatordoc.aspx?i=75

3 American Academy of Arts and Sciences, *Public Research Universities: Understanding the Financial Model* (Cambridge, Mass., 2016), the Lincoln Project: Excellence and Access in Public Higher Education, www.amacad.org/LincolnProject.

4 Nancy F. Cott, "Money Talks," *American Historian*, May 2016.

5 Charles A. Lindbergh, "Aviation, Geography, and Race," *Reader's Digest*, Nov. 1939.

Gretchen Sullivan Sorin

The Future of History: Egg Rolls, Egg Creams and Empanadas

WITH THE OPENING in September 2016 of the Smithsonian's new museum of African American history in Washington, D.C., record crowds descended on the building to see the exhibitions. By March 24, 2017, the six-month anniversary of the opening, 1.3 million visitors—most using the timed-entry tickets—had entered its doors. The tickets remain the most difficult to obtain in the city.

New York City's Museum at Eldridge Street (located in a former Lower East Side synagogue) holds an annual history-themed festival called Egg Rolls, Egg Creams and Empanadas that fills the local streets with people anxious to learn about Jewish, Chinese, and Puerto Rican foods, crafts, music, and culture as well as the neighborhood that supported all three groups.

A quick search of the web indicates a considerable number of comments and discussions about the various tours and experiences at New York's Tenement Museum, and potential visitors inquire online about the best way to obtain tickets for their popular tours.

And although the president urged theater-goers to boycott the musical *Hamilton*, ticket sales have been brisk, and regularly sell out.

Gretchen Sullivan Sorin is the Director and Distinguished Professor of the Cooperstown Graduate Program. She has served as a consultant to many museums and as a guest curator for numerous exhibitions. Dr. Sorin has written and lectured extensively on African American history and museum practice.

It would seem that in many quarters public interest in history is alive and well—but whose history? And, as the enthusiasm for these programs might indicate, perhaps the way that audiences prefer their history presented is changing.

Roy Rosenzweig and David Thelen published their study of the "popular uses of history in American life," called *The Presence of the Past*, in 1998. The national survey found that Americans viewed museums as the most trustworthy purveyors of history, considerably more reliable, in their opinion, than books, high school teachers, and even relatives who had experienced past events. Academic historians—college professors—were notably a part of this group, but considered less trustworthy than museums with only 54.3 percent of respondents rating them between 8 and 10 on the authors' trustworthiness scale of 1 to 10. The individuals who responded to the survey felt more disconnected from history when it was presented in classrooms or on movie screens, but they found that the authenticity of history museums, the opportunity to see the real thing or experience places where historic events happened, seemed much more tangible and believable. Participants in the study found "history" boring, equating it with those deadly classes in high school that we all remember. But they found "the past" fascinating, particularly as it related in some way to their own or their families' lives. Education builds on something familiar, and perhaps this relationship to the personal enables visitors more readily to respond to and absorb history that is relevant and personally meaningful.

More recent research by Reach Advisors provided similar findings.[1] Their study identified history museums as the most dependable source of information on history. On a trustworthiness scale of 0 to 10 with 0 equal to not at all trustworthy, history museums earned a score of 6.7, while academic historians scored 5.7, making historians equally as believable as Wikipedia!

It seems as if the future of history, or at least the public understanding of it, may be squarely in the hands of public historians—as long as we don't squander this incredible opportunity to offer something valuable to current and potential museum audiences. Being the people's most trusted supplier of history is a tremendous responsibility. If the public trusts us as their source of truths about the past, we must be responsible for making sure that the information we provide is broadly representative, easily accessible, and useful.

The vast majority of history museums in the United States are historic houses. Some have recreated themselves in the face of changing demographics, changing technology, and ever more diverse communities, but most historic house museums have failed to adjust to the needs of twenty-first-century audiences. Professionalization, in some ways, hurts public engagement, pushing people further and further away from more authentic recreations of the past and into stale, never-changing period rooms and dry "lectures," called tours, that often focus on the distinctness and rarity of artifacts rather than on the cultures and people that produced them. Such "talking at" the visitor remains the norm at so many historic sites. During a recent historic house tour, one visitor noted that the guide's most memorable remarks centered around the shortness of the bed and the chiming of the French clock: "it still works," he commented, and then sounded the bell. Sadly, many historic site tours include precious little actual history and nothing that one might find useful to modern audiences. Exceptional adulation for the lifestyles of the rich and famous, the unspoken theme of many historic houses, strikes a chord in the voyeur in each of us, but it is not particularly life enriching. Admittedly, these houses pose an interpretive problem for historians. It is difficult to discuss Susan B. Anthony's role in the suffrage movement or her effect on women's rights today within her domestic space. Similarly, conversations concerning Jay Gould's unethical business practices as a prototypical robber baron and the way that his excesses changed governmental regulations are challenging while standing in his private chambers at Lyndhurst. While it is easier said than done, historic house museums must alter the way they think about their sacred period spaces and their missions to get at the core reasons that visitors should come to these sites (besides entertainment and voyeurism). Whether the added value is in learning about the history of women's rights, slavery, immigration, ethical business practices, nature conservation, or democracy, there can be broad American values and themes underpinning these historic places, if only we uncover them and figure out how to relate them to museum audiences in active, participatory ways.

MAKING HISTORY BROADLY REPRESENTATIVE

I recently brought a group of museum studies students of color together with several museum professionals who wanted to consider how to make their institutions more accessible to both millennials and people of color. A vice president at a large history museum asked, "Can we just do programs for them, or do we have to have them on our staff?" This rather appalling, although not intentionally bigoted, statement suggests that at least this museum, and I suspect many others, has a long way to go in thinking about creating truly inclusive institutions. In many places, inclusion means finding ways of bringing "them" into "our" institution instead of working collaboratively and doing the hard work of recreating an institution of value to everyone. Unfortunately, there is no reason to assume that the racial divide that exists in the nation does not exist in history museums. Do museum staffs really want to change their institutions, or do they expect that a few token programs to engage community members will convert new and more diverse audiences into regular supporters?

As the demographics of the nation change, if the audiences who visit history museums and the staff who work in them fail to keep pace with these changes, many of these institutions will cease to exist from lack of interest or visitation. Perhaps we should be asking why the history that we are telling and the experiences we are offering often no longer resonate with the audiences we seek to attract.

There is endless talk about diversity in American museums. Diversity and inclusion have become the topics of conferences, the covers of professional magazines, and more recently the subject of entire journals. Diversity-talk has been an ever-increasing drumbeat in the history museum sphere for decades. As early as the 1960s, leaders in the profession were discussing the importance of expanding the diversity of the field. Louis C. Jones, director of the New York Historical

Association and founder of the Cooperstown Graduate Program, offered an important and strongly worded statement in a keynote address at the American Association of Museums meeting in 1969. "I see black janitors and guards; once in a while in the big city museums I see a black docent," he said, "but aside from that the jobs all belong to whitey."[2] In response to this diversity-talk, many history museums have experimented with programs and exhibitions that seek to include broader audiences.

We know that the lack of people of color in professional positions and as board members, and thus in the decision-making roles of the museum, is one concern. But the typical approach that history museums take to diversity is to tinker around the edges—to offer one-off programs, plan Black History Month programs in February followed by Women's History Month programs in March, or add mentions of slavery to the same old plantation tour. Real inclusion means looking at every aspect of the institution's history, board, operations, and programming and thinking broadly about the stories the museum tells from the ground up.

MAKING HISTORY MORE ACCESSIBLE?

Recently, a group of women gathered at the local library in Inwood, a largely Dominican neighborhood in upper Manhattan, to hear the presentation of an educator from the Dyckman Farmhouse Alliance, the neighborhood history museum. Literacy, Inc. convened the meeting. The women were largely Spanish speaking, although a few of them were Middle Eastern. They spoke of their desire to provide positive educational experiences for their children, but they did not see museum-going as an option. They did not perceive history museums as places where they were welcome or that they could afford to visit. Museums are just too expensive, they said. Justifying their admission fees, museum staff members often note that entrance fees to a museum are less than the cost of a night at the movies, but the families that need museums the most may not be going to the movies.

The women in the Inwood literacy group did not understand the concept of suggested donations, the policy at many museums that enables you to pay what you can afford. They thought they were required to pay the price on the sign for admittance. While the women expressed the need for and their interest in educational enrichment for their children and were aware of the potential of museums to provide such experiences—for other people—they did not see them as an option for their own families. But they were particularly excited to discover a Spanish-speaking educator from a history museum in their own neighborhood, someone who sought them out and invited them to bring their children to the museum at no charge. This is, of course, an anecdotal experience, but perhaps it is also a parable. So many museums complain that they have been unable to bring minority and underserved audiences through their doors on a regular basis. But how many of them have taken the time to seek out and listen to the needs of the people they could serve? How many have provided bilingual interpreters or guides who can help visitors negotiate the museum's interior? Museums create elite spaces with specific rules of behavior to which not everyone is privy. Then we wonder why broader audiences do not take advantage of them.

Not every potential audience knows how to use a museum once they enter the front door. What do you do? What are the rules? Cool Culture, an organization founded by educators in New York City, provides access for low-income families to arts, scientific, and other cultural institutions. Their teachers work with cross-generational family groups to insure that visitors are not intimidated by museum spaces. And, for special programs, they welcome their participants at the door. The Cool Culture passport provides more than fifty thousand families with free admission to ninety museums and cultural institutions throughout the city. Cool Culture offers outstanding programs in their member museums in English, Spanish, and Chinese, and their research shows that their families become regular museumgoers and often visit more frequently than the museum's conventional audience.[3]

Twenty-five years after *Excellence and Equity*, we are still discussing how to provide environments that enable us to welcome visitors beyond the traditional elite museum audiences and to keep them coming back. Some museums have closed and others have merged. Is this an indication of a lack of interest in history, or is it the natural winnowing out of history businesses that are not responsive to their audiences and therefore no longer viable or needed?

MAKING HISTORY USEFUL

History museums and historic sites have a civic responsibility. They have the ability to help visitors become well-informed citizens who understand the processes of government and have the tools to make thoughtful decisions about community issues. Using artifacts and documents, museums can teach visitors how to evaluate evidence and determine its veracity, understand the way that American democracy works and when it has failed to work, and how to make informed voting choices. But, of course, to fulfill these goals the museum must have sufficient public appeal to attract visitors and hopefully keep them coming back as well as the business acumen to enable the museum to survive. All of this must be done while making the presentation, whatever its form—exhibition, program, historic site interpretation, dialogue, school field trip—entertaining. For museums, useful history (history the person who learns it can use in their daily lives) changes with community and societal needs.

Consider these examples of programs that engage new visitors and are useful because they address issues that matter in people's lives today:

The Detroit Historical Society decided to address the city's long-standing controversy over the civil unrest of the 1960s by facing this difficult history head-on. *Detroit 67: Looking Back to Move Forward*, a community-wide effort with one hundred partners throughout the city, is an ambitious and experimental undertaking that includes gathering oral histories, a ground-breaking exhibition, discussions, workshops, and other programs that consider Detroit's past from 1917 and its future through 2067. Community members and scholars will be sharing the process of historical documentation. The planners hope that the project will "create a 'model' that makes history relevant to a community's present and future."[4]

An exhibition developed by the Smithsonian Institution Traveling Exhibition Service called *Becoming American: Teenagers and Immigration* invites viewers to examine compelling portraits of immigrants and interviews with teens who came from Latin America, the Caribbean, Europe, Africa, the Middle East, and Asia. The exhibition documents contemporary experiences of immigration and encourages viewers to consider their own hopes of becoming American.

The Lower East Side Tenement Museum realized that many of the children visiting the site lived in tenement buildings very similar to the museum's site and that many of their apartments did not meet the New York City building code. In order to incorporate that insight into their outreach, the museum staff developed a program that taught these students about tenement life in the past and then gave them the tools to become building inspectors today. The students learned how to inspect their family's apartments and how to talk to their landlords.

Concerned about the large number of men of color in prison, Eastern State Penitentiary in Philadelphia, which closed as a prison in 1971 and opened as a historic site in 1990, created an exhibition entitled *Considering Mass Incarceration*. The exhibition features a larger-than-life-size information graphic that visually depicts incarceration around the world and highlights the United States at the very top of the list. The site was founded in the eighteenth century, in the wake of the birth of American democracy, by enlightenment thinkers, including Benjamin Franklin, who expressed concern about prison reform. Eastern State grew out of this concern. Today, the museum's mission is to interpret the history of the site, but it also extends beyond that to examine the history, effectiveness, and fairness of the American justice system. Discussions and forums about corrections and contemporary issues related to the justice system are a significant part of their programming. Truly committed to diversity and inclusion, Eastern State recently hired formerly incarcerated inmates to be tour guides in the museum.

The Dyckman Farmhouse Museum in the northern Manhattan community of Inwood is an eighteenth-century New Netherland farmhouse in the middle of a neighborhood that is now more than 65 percent Dominican.[5] The historic site provides visitors with a welcoming green space, but the museum staff has recreated the period house and grounds to focus on issues related to agriculture, immigration, family, and literacy. The period rooms become merely stage sets for storytelling or discussions of topics both past and present. Labels, the website, and all program publications are in both English and Spanish. The house also showcases the art of the neighborhood, including responses by Dominican artists to the local Dutch heritage. The museum determined that enrichment for children was a community need that could be supported by the garden and a summer camp that focused on learning about food and nutrition. Providing a daily program as well as a healthy Dominican lunch for students also greatly assisted working parents in the neighborhood.

The event on the Lower East Side begins with klezmer music and dancing up and down Eldridge Street, followed by Mambo music, Chinese Opera, Puerto Rican mask-making, and dozens of craft and food sampling activities that highlight the culture of three of the neighborhood's prominent communities. Sitting side-by-side, a Jewish scribe and a Chinese calligrapher practice their crafts. The annual Eggs Rolls, Egg Creams and Empanadas Festival, now a signature of the Museum at Eldridge Street, brings more than ten thousand people from all over the city together to share one another's cultures and learn about New York's diversity.[6]

So where do we go from here?

If only historic sites could figure out how to broaden the stories they tell to include the connections between past and present. Obviously the links are there, if we choose to make use of them. We need to show people how the past affects the present and connects us to the future.

Museum missions must change to identify core ideas that they can interpret and community needs that they can address. Public history in museums and historic sites goes beyond artifacts—indeed, museums are not about artifacts, but about people. Artifacts are the props of history, but people are the reason that museums exist. History museums need to experiment more and fear risk less. Public dialogues, computer simulations, ESL classes, citizenship training, cross-cultural events, sip and learn programs, immersive programs—whatever it takes to make history relevant and interesting—are fair game.

We need to learn to listen to our communities and engage them in the process of telling history, rather than simply telling them what we want them to know. We need to share authority with our constituents and let go of total curatorial control.

Museums must commit resources (time, planning, and especially money) to broad institutional change, not just diversity-talk, to develop institutions that are truly more inclusive.

So, what is the future of history? It is finally time to address, forthrightly and systemically, the issues of equity and inclusion discussed in this essay. Over the course of American history, minority groups and women have played a significant part in pushing democracy forward. As an African American woman and museum professional, I ask that my colleagues do what they know is right—make their museums, their staffs, their boards, and the history they present representative, accessible, and usable.

As a historian and professor of history museum studies, I see enthusiastic, young historians each year who are determined to use history as a vehicle for social change and who look at history as a way to help Americans understand themselves and their world. They are determined to change museums and to make them more responsive to the communities they serve. They are the future of history, and I think we are leaving it in capable hands.

---

1 Reach Advisors, "Public Perceptions of Trustworthiness," *Museum*, Nov.–Dec. 2015, p. 7.

2 Quoted in William S. Walker, "Cooperstown and the Radical Tradition of Folk History," essay in forthcoming volume on the "radical roots" of history. This is part of a collaborative research project led by Denise Meringolo, University of Maryland—Baltimore County. See also William S. Walker, "Folklore and the Roots of Public History Training in Cooperstown," Feb. 3, 2017, *History@Work*, http://ncph.org/history-at-work/folklore-and-the-roots-of-public-history-training-in-cooperstown.

3 Cool Culture research cited by Cool Culture Executive Director Candace Anderson at the Cooperstown Graduate Program Professional Seminar, Spring 2016.

4 Detroit 67 Project, Detroit Historical Society, https://detroithistorical.org.

5 "Northern Zone, South of the Border Flavor," *New York Times*, Feb. 27, 2009.

6 "The Egg Rolls and Egg Creams Festival," Dec. 16, 2014, Mapping Yiddish New York, https://myny.ccnmtl.columbia.edu/content/egg-rolls-and-egg-creams-festival.

Debra Block   History Education in the (Mis)Information Age

"Convinced that the people are the only safe depositories of their own liberty, and that they are not safe unless enlightened to a certain degree, I have looked on our present state of liberty as a short-lived possession unless the mass of the people could be informed to a certain degree."

—Thomas Jefferson (1805)[1]

"Get your facts first, and then you can distort them as much as you please."

—Mark Twain (1890)[2]

AS EDUCATORS, we periodize history, using such terms as *the Renaissance, Reconstruction,* and *imperialism*. Labels like these are intended to frame students' understanding of the past, creating a coherent whole from the unwieldy parts and fostering an appreciation of the ways in which this amalgam is usually both greater and lesser than the sum total. The reality that there is diversity of experience in any given time

Debra Block is an historian and educational consultant. After twenty years in the classroom, she has spent the last fifteen combining her scholarly understanding and educational skills to write curricula, evaluate programs, and provide professional development to educators. She also works in a curatorial role on exhibitions, taking materials "from the archive to the rug." The one common thread to all of these endeavors has been the great privilege to learn from every experience.

span, i.e., there are many valid although often omitted truths, further disturbs a tidy approach to historical inquiry.

Today, we say that we are living in the "Information Age," again a shorthand that probably masks more than it reveals. A democratic society thrives on access to information, and in the pre-Internet era, as we all understood, the greater the access to information, the better. Tyranny resulted when information was manipulated or not freely available. Given the current spectrum of news and information, from truth to falsehood, we see that the dynamic has shifted. Access is no longer the issue; determining accuracy is. If this task is difficult for adults, imagine the confusion for children (and those who teach them).

How do we help students of all ages make sense of, process, understand all with which we are bombarded? How does an abundance of information become an educational tool rather than an obstacle to deep and meaningful engagement? History education far too often is the victim of a litany of facts and figures. Data swamps us. Not that the goals associated with evaluating tables and graphs are any less essential or laudable. But I witness the challenge of coping with a flood of both qualitative and quantitative data on a daily basis in my current role as a consultant who provides professional development for educators and writes and edits curricula. It is imperative to train our youngest minds to navigate the onslaught of information and develop the ability to evaluate what they receive.

NO ONE UNDERSTOOD this need more than Thomas Jefferson. An educated citizenry was (and is) vital to a republican form of government. Truth was the essence of his understanding of the principles of the Enlightenment: "We hold these truths to be self-evident, that all men are created equal."[3]

One wonders if truth is still self-evident. This question stems from two realities, one frightening and the other heartening. Misinformation abounds. On the upside, individuals often have truths distinct from broader societal understandings. Perspective and bias affect our sense of the truth, and there are indeed multiple realities that we must consider. But if we are going to make choices, the essence of a republican form of government, then we need information beyond our personal worldview. Likewise, if we are going to select representatives to make the choices for us, we need to know who they are. A culture of commonly accepted facts, about which we may disagree, is the foundation of democracy. The ebb and flow of information is essential.

Today it is not enough to get information. We must make sense of it and assess its validity. It is far too late to acquire these critical skills as an adult or even in college. Training children in higher-order thinking skills is essential and very much in vogue in the K–12 universe. I'd like to put in a plug for some basic-order thinking skills as well. And facts. Children, like the adults around them, are quick with opinions, far too often not grounded in verifiable details. The proper cognitive path, ensconced in the scientific method, is that opinions should stem from observation, an assertion I make with confidence after more than twenty years in the classroom, training students to think critically and write effectively. Alas, we currently revel in a world where every opinion is valid. This unchallenged assertion of ungrounded supposition is distinct from genuine differences in truth that result from varied experience that naturally generates disparate realities, e.g. the antebellum South was quite distinct for slaves and owners, to say nothing of the divisions within each group.

The role of education is to develop the skills to process truth and determine the reliability of sources. This goal holds for both contemporary and historical information. Indeed, one of the most pressing objectives is to see the connection between the past and present, the essential "how did we get here?" The waters become muddied when we think we are better informed than we are. School administrators often tell me that there is no need to cover historical facts with students: "It is all on their phones." Presuming availability and access to information, they encourage those experiences that develop the ability to analyze, contextualize, and compare what they have already assumed to be a sound body of material. But what if the information is inaccurate or insufficient? Do students have the ability to make these determinations? While the Internet is the great connector and a potential agent for genuine democracy, it is proving to be an even better platform for manipulation.

How do we determine truth in this era of overwhelming information and misinformation? The first step is to acknowledge the complexity of truth; it is often multifaceted and usually paradoxical. Here, education is essential to train children to process a rich and varied past. As long as history education is no more than facts and figures and dates, attaining this goal is unlikely. I strongly advocate a "less is more" approach. If one wants students to understand that the relationship between business and government is a complex one—that *laissez faire* doesn't exist when Congress sets tariffs, enforces regulations, and designates transportation routes, for example—one can gingerly hope that memorizing a litany of laws will lead them to that ultimate conclusion. Or one can dig deep into a few items—the Smoot-Hawley Tariff Act, the Northwest Ordinance, and the Meat Inspection Act. So the administrators aren't wrong. The information *is* at students' fingertips, but they need to be educated in how to use and make sense of it. As do their teachers. They must learn how to distinguish valid information from tripe. They have to be trained to build an argument from information, not fish for that which supports predetermined opinions.

A more perfect union results from the ability to identify the truth. During the opening scene of the HBO series *The Newsroom*, the anti-hero responds to a college student's question regarding the greatness of America. In his profanity-laced rant, he happens upon one irrefutable and essential truth: we were great and what made us great "was that we were informed."[4]

The time he refers to was different from today in terms of both access to and abundance of information. In 2017, we run the gamut from fact-lite to deliberate lies, inconsistencies, inaccuracies, and the most recent entry into the landscape: alternative facts. Truth is not a matter of popularity. Historical knowledge is not subject to a vote. As Henry David Thoreau noted, "any man more right than his neighbors constitutes a majority of one already."[5]

The abundance of information has resulted in an increased siloization. The acquisition of knowledge reinforces the views we already hold. Factionalism has existed since antiquity, but the massive amount of information available convinces us of our certainty and the equal wrongness of those with whom we disagree. Absent commonly accepted information, we become armed camps with artilleries of facts and figures. The Internet allows us to customize our bubbles, consuming information from those with whom we already agree.

The very nature of truth has changed. As contemporary discourse questions and challenges the legitimacy of all information, it is a seamless transfer to dispute the historic record as well. It is easy to deny facts in evidence because we can find material to refute just about anything. Michelle Obama marvels that she lives in a house built by slaves and Bill O'Reilly produces the payment receipts to said slaves. An absence of agreement on historical facts widens the chasm. The inability of facts to change people's opinions has resulted in the "power of belief over evidence."[6]

Whether or not this new reality was inevitable given the proliferation of information it is too soon to say and beyond the scope of this essay. Years of blame, calling into question the legitimacy of mainstream media outlets, have resulted in the elimination of gatekeepers of the truth. Misinformation/lies/propaganda are not new, but the extent of their proliferation is. Information manipulated, as Plato feared, is a path to tyranny. Perhaps the form has changed, so demagogues no longer need to control content, but its flow. The expression "seeing is believing" has been replaced with "Googling is believing."[7]

Education could (and can) stem the tide to make the next generation of information consumers critical about what they receive and use to make sense of the past. Education shapes and reflects our society. It is a repository of our values, ideals, aspirations. The classroom is the place where the silos can be breached. Again, Jefferson provides inspiration: "I look to the diffusion of light and education as the resource most to be relied on for ameliorating the conditions, promoting the virtue and advancing the happiness of man."[8]

Jefferson is a good illustration of the problems and opportunities of history education. There is an exhibition at the new National Museum of African American History and Culture, *The Paradox of Liberty*. The president is surrounded with the names of some of his slaves on bricks. The building blocks of our nation are literally the coexistence of his ideals and his reality. Helping students make sense of these contradictions, of the ability to feel and act in ways that seem to negate one another, is the essence of historical inquiry. Jefferson's truth is no more or less valid than that of the slaves on his plantation and both are necessary to understanding our past. What is not legitimate is falsehood. History education, properly done, can help us make these distinctions and serve as a bulwark against the unsubstantiated. Paradox yes. Untruth no.

There are many reasons for lamenting the current state of history education. As one recent cartoon quipped, "those who don't study history are doomed to repeat it. Yet those who *do* study history are doomed to stand by helplessly while everyone else repeats it." We need our students to know and value accuracy. We need to respect, acknowledge, and reward the way the brain works—observation and information first, conclusion second.

Studying the past and teaching it are also two distinct kinds of work. Academics take time and distance to see long-term causes and effects, and consider different paths to understanding. K–12 educators do not have the luxury of time as they combine instruction in skills, content, and discipline. They need to help their students make sense of current events and establish the lens through which their students comprehend the past. This has long been my own professional paradox—how to bring the sensibilities of the historian to the immediacy of the classroom.

Teachers are instructed to build lessons around content and language objectives—the *what* and *how* of what they teach. This simple schema is useful for considering the current state of K–12 history education. *What* do we want them to learn and *how* do we want them to learn it? Yet these simple questions exist in the deeply varied landscape in which K–12 history instruction happens. The first variable is time. In every training I do, the most common lament is the absence of time—to teach, to plan, to engage with colleagues, to reflect on instructional practice.

Recent studies confirm what we knew anecdotally. No Child Left Behind (NCLB) obliterated social studies education in the K–5 universe. In some schools, the instructional time dedicated to history, civics, and geography declined by more than 70 percent. This result is not surprising. The mandate of the 2002 law was for literacy and math. States establish licensure requirements and most do not require competence in content areas such as history or science for elementary educators. So teachers defer to that which they know and understand best, spending more time preparing students for tests that will "prove" educational gains. That social studies content is a wonderful way to fulfill the NCLB mandates gets lost in the practical reality of teacher preference and comfort. This limited exposure in the elementary grades has come home to roost in the secondary school world, where students enter without a meaningful foundation.[9]

There is enormous variation across the land. All fifty states maintain some level of commitment to history education and have graduation requirements that span from a general requirement to specific evaluations in U.S. history and civics. The December 2016 report of the Education Commission of the States provides a comprehensive overview of the graduation requirements and testing in history education for all fifty states. While they all mandate a minimum number of course hours, they vary in terms of specifics and evaluation. Most states require at least three courses in history and stipulate the number of credits for U.S. and state history. Some include a citizenship test for high school graduation. While most states set these mandates, some do not specify course content. A few states test as early as third grade, but most include testing on the secondary level only. One way to fulfill these mandates is to place a high percentage of the grade on end-of-course final examinations. These metrics convey what students have been taught, but the real purpose of evaluation should be to provide a guide for the future, not a recounting of the past.[10]

Content has long been a contentious arena. Should K–12 social studies education be a primer on citizenship and patriotism? If so, who defines what is patriotic—pledging allegiance to the flag or burning it? Is omission censorship, as some opponents claim? Or can it help students understand that by choosing some items over others we are mirroring the genuine process of how people lived their lives? They certainly did not compartmentalize and their identities at work, home, school, and church were intertwined.

One possible model of common ground is the revised examination for U.S. citizenship that the Immigration and Naturalization Service administers. The product of an intense revision in the years after the attacks of 9/11, these one hundred questions define essential knowledge. We can specify what everyone should know. If an immigrant cannot become a citizen of this country without mastering one hundred basic facts, those who are born here should be held to the same standard. But much is politicized. Critics of the Common Core claim that the government mandates content when the real problem of these standards is their absence of content specificity. Sure, students are supposed to substantiate claims with evidence, but precious few curriculum materials are provided as models for how best to do that.

Part of the concern resides with how history is taught. Even where teachers emphasize content in service to bigger ideas and interdisciplinary skill development, they tend to fall into the unit-by-unit chronological trajectory. Educators are reluctant to skip content, and "covering" the materials takes precedence over truly understanding it, as "the parade" of history often obscures more than it reveals. Judicious parsing of content, however, can be quite effective in balancing the interplay of ideas, information, and skills.

Again, based on my decades in the classroom, I can comfortably assert that history education works best when topics are divided into manageable bites. Students can untangle the pieces, master them, and then put them together in a coherent analysis. Such "jigsaws" and other cooperative learning strategies actively engage students as they take overship of their learning. Make them responsible for teaching others what they know and critical thinking develops.

Division of content is not an endorsement of simplification. Rather than sanitize we should embrace our complex truths. Form can follow function. We need to make choices about our content. History is about choices—what choices existed, who got to make them, and the impact of the choices on future endeavors. We need to let students see the connections, overlaps, and gaps so they will appreciate how the past can be used to think about what happened and make sense of the present.

If we are going to teach children how to study the past, we need to acknowledge these realities. This does not mean history class becomes the time of doom and gloom. Students intuit that even within their classroom, individuals experience the same events differently. Using this lens as a foundation, children can explore bias and inequity. And classrooms, where children make decisions in groups, are the ideal place to teach lessons of politics, civics, and government.

We must emphasize process over acquisition of information. Testing, should it be used, can serve as frequent checks along the path of this growth rather than an all-encompassing evaluation that yields little in the way of future direction for learning. Questions can be creative, extending from the information students have in front of them to ways to extrapolate about the human experience. Acquisition of knowledge is both receptive and expressive—think reading and writing. Both can be opportunities for active learning.

We need history standards that incorporate the complex relationship today's youth has with the truth. There are opportunities for children, receptive and impressively committed to their perceptions of fairness, that make educational settings the perfect place to build a foundation of respect for the search for truth. In classes, students learn best by doing. They can partner with public history, as museum collections can be brought into classrooms via technology. They can take virtual tours around the globe.

Eliminating the silos of the adult world before they become ossified is essential. Rather than dividing content into distinct classes, the Common Core provides bridges. The brain does not function in such discrete ways, so why do we educate children as if they think about biology, art, and math, for example, in fifty-two-minute increments? Perhaps the skills need to be subdivided, but the content must be fluid. Historical inquiry can and should be made relevant across all academic disciplines, beginning with student awareness of self and community and extending to an appreciation of how all of these disciplines shaped the events of the past.

We must create opportunities for active learning through exploration of and connection to the global community. Inculcating accountability for words and deeds might allow the next generation to have a different relationship with the truth and employ their access to abundant information in ways that are genuine and beneficial.

The tide does seem to be turning. Many schools are adopting the 3C standards of the National Conference on Social Studies.[11] New state standards in places like California and Connecticut are integrating analysis with salient information, establishing the appropriate connection between information and understanding. This push has been heartened by the Every Student Succeeds Act, passed in December 2015, which specifically identifies the need for American history and civics education.[12]

Tests could actually help here as long as they are the means and not the ends. They could identify what information and concepts students retain. They could help us shape the neural pathways if we reward acquisition of information and point us towards meaningful next steps. History properly taught creates critical thinkers. We don't need to do more. We need to do it better. We need to help children assess the context/bias/perspective of what they encounter. We need an engaged citizenry and an informed one. We need those who can distinguish between fact, fiction, fantasy, wishes, and lies.

At the same time, we must acknowledge the complexity and diversity of truth. The study of history is about the paradoxes, connections, and confusions of the past. The teaching of it should be as well.

---

1 Thomas Jefferson to Littleton Waller Tazewell, Jan. 5, 1805, Founders Online, National Archives and Records Administration, http://founders.archives.gov/documents/Jefferson/99-01-02-0958.

2 Rudyard Kipling, "An Interview with Mark Twain," *From Sea to Sea: Letters of Travel* (New York, 1899), 180. The piece was first published as a newspaper article in 1890.

3 Declaration of Independence, 1776.

4 Aaron Sorkin, "We Just Decided To," *The Newsroom*, season 1, episode 1 (HBO, aired June 24, 2012).

5 Henry David Thoreau, "Civil Disobedience" (1849), *Hypertexts*, American Studies at the University of Virginia, http://xroads.virginia.edu/~hyper2/thoreau/civil.html, based on the same in *The Writings of Henry David Thoreau* (Boston, 1906), 3:356–387 (quotation 369).

6 Michael Shermer, "How to Convince Someone When Facts Fail," *Scientific American*, Jan. 1, 2017, www.scientificamerican.com/article/how-to-convince-someone-when-facts-fail.

7 Michael P. Lynch, "Googling Is Believing," *New York Times*, March 9, 2016.

8 Thomas Jefferson to Cornelius Camden Blatchly, Oct. 21, 1822, Founders Online, http://founders.archives.gov/documents/Jefferson/98-01-02-3106.

9 Kathleen Babini, "Has Elementary Social Studies Become Collateral Damage of the No Child Left Behind Act?" (PhD diss., Northeastern University, 2013), https://repository.library.northeastern.edu/files/neu:1077.

10 Education Commission of the States, *50-State Comparison: Civic Education Policies*, www.ecs.org/citizenship-education-policies; Education Commission of the States, *Companion Report: 50-State Comparison: Civic Education*, www.ecs.org/companion-report-50-state-comparison-civic-education.

11 National Council for the Social Studies, College, Career, and Civic Life (C3) Framework for Social Studies State Standards, www.socialstudies.org/c3.

12 Every Student Succeeds Act, www.congress.gov/bill/114th-congress/senate-bill/1177. See Title II, Part B—National Activities, Subpart 3: American History and Civics Education, which identifies and funds initiatives on the state level.

Manisha Sinha   History and Its Discontents

IN SURVEYING THE FIELD of history today, one cannot help but be struck, with due apologies to Freud, by its discontents. My purpose here is not to address the timeless question "What is history?" except perhaps in a tangential manner. Nor am I interested in tracing the evolution of history as an academic discipline from a sort of Rankian (after the famous German historian Leopold von Ranke) positivist subject, mainly the reporting of facts, to a more self-conscious field, where the interpretations, proclivities, and contexts of historians become an essential part of considering the facts that they have uncovered. Only the most simple and simplistic views of history would regard the subject as the mere accumulation and regurgitation of facts. Though, of course, facts matter—historians may be entitled to their own interpretations but not their own evidence. History, then, is not so much a matter of the mere collection of facts as it is a matter of what facts count, how we choose to organize and present them, and who our intended audiences are. Ideas matter, as von Ranke's contemporary antagonist, the German philosopher G. W. F. Hegel, insisted.[1] History, then, lies at the cusp of the humanities and the social sciences. Its

Manisha Sinha is the Draper Chair in American History at the University of Connecticut. She is the author most recently of *The Slave's Cause: A History of Abolition*, long-listed for the National Book Awards and awarded the Avery Craven Prize by the Organization of American Historians. She currently is working on a book on Reconstruction.

status as evidence-based, analytical narrative gives it a special role in informing and engaging broader audiences outside academe.

It is precisely this role that has generated controversy over history's definition and boundaries, or over what counts as history, particularly in the United States. Since history was traditionally conceived of as informing national identities, it has always been fodder for political debate. Most of the recent controversies over what constitutes historical knowledge are traceable to the rise and proliferation of the new histories (now not so new) and the ascendancy of social history since the 1960s. Influenced by the Civil Rights, women's, and anti-war movements, the effort to write history from the "bottom up" has virtually revolutionized U.S. history. The emergence of new areas of inquiry—African American, women's, Native American, Latino, and Asian American history, and more recently the history of sexuality—essentially histories of people who had been left out of mainstream historical narratives, has redefined the contours and content of American history. Many of these subfields have now matured and possess their own paradigms and issues and cannot be viewed as mere additions to pre-existing accounts of U.S. history. They attempt not simply to add people left out of history or displace others, such as the Founding Fathers, as has been contended, but to present a more complex, holistic, and nuanced view of American history.

Yet their place and findings in American history remain contested, as the highly charged debates over the new national history standards in the 1990s revealed. Lynn Cheney, the former head of the National Endowment for the Humanities, contended that they were inspired by a "great hatred of traditional history." While that controversy has died down, it lives on in contemporary debates over "political correctness."[2] The incorporation of some of the new social histories into the work of public history, museums, and historic sites, including markers maintained by the National Park Service, reveals that the battle may have been largely won even though it continues to generate backlash. In short, the histories of ordinary Americans—women, immigrants, workers, Native and African Americans, to name a few—are finally getting their due. The recent opening and unprecedented success of the Smithsonian's National Museum of African American History and Culture in Washington, D.C., mark the culmination of this trend.

In most cases, the emergence of the new histories has not just meant the addition of areas of study but also a change in methodology and subject matter in already established historical fields, like the new political and economic histories. These changes reflect not only the bottom-up approach but also the borrowing of social science methods, which characterizes much of recent social history. For instance, the use of quantitative methods led to an entirely new term for quantitative history, Cliometrics. Computers, digitization of previously inaccessible historical sources, and databases have led to a technological revolution in historical methodology as scholars have been able to mine census records, newspapers, city directories, and other sources to an extent not previously possible. Such methods have been especially helpful in studying the history of common folk, who did not leave behind extensive written records. In my field of slavery and abolition studies, the development of the Trans-Atlantic Slave Trade Database housed at Emory University and the slave narratives website at the University of North Carolina, Chapel Hill, has proven to be invaluable. They also allow amateur historians and an interested lay public to get access to historical research more easily. Dealing with the silence of the archives when it comes to recovering the histories of women, Native Americans, African Americans, and most common folk has also forced historians to become more innovative in both theory and method. Innovations within historical methodology like the use of non-traditional oral sources, including the spoken word as well as music, and material and artwork have further contributed to what can only be called the expansion of history in method and scope. It is highly ironic, then, that some today would question the value of history precisely at the moment of its greatest expansion.

The new American history is broad based and interdisciplinary—and not just in terms of method. Theoretical perspectives like anthropologist Clifford Geertz's notion of culture as "webs of significance" became very popular among social historians in the 1970s and 1980s. The cultural turn in history may have run its course, but it continues to inform social and intellectual history. The most significant theoretical innovations came from across the Atlantic. Several decades ago, James A. Henretta of the University of Maryland identified the French Annalistes and British Marxists as the two dominant theoretical influences on the new social history.[3] Certainly, American social historians attempted to emulate the *Annales* School in France, which arose in the 1920s. Following Annalistes such as Marc Bloch, Ferdinand Braudel, and Emmanuel Le Roy Ladurie, they became more concerned with the economic and social rather than the political, with the social and "geo-economic" space rather than the nation-state. In a sense, they anticipated the rise of environmental history, historical geography, and doing history in the Anthropocene, our current preoccupations. Like natural scientists, who have led the intellectual and political battle against climate change deniers, perhaps it is about time that historians bring valuable historical perspectives to the debate over global warming.[4]

In some areas of American history, such as the history of slavery, labor, and women and gender, the influence of British Marxism has been defining, particularly the work of Christopher Hill, historian of the English Civil War; E. P. Thompson's iconic *The Making of the English Working Class*; and the works of Eric J. Hobsbawm. Neo-Marxist thinkers such as Antonio Gramsci and Jurgen Habermas and postmodern theories from Foucault to Baudrillard continue to inform the work of historians. The attempt to center people who were at the margins in historical narratives—artisans, workers, slaves, small farmers, and the subaltern—in many cases went hand-in-hand with the use of Marxist and neo-Marxist theories. This was true not just of U.S. history but also of the colonial and postcolonial histories of Asia, Africa, and Latin America. Combined with the political influence of the 1960s social movements, theoretical radicalism produced strong oppositional accounts of U.S. history that rejected the conventional, linear, and Whiggish understanding of American history as the always-expanding account of freedom and democracy. Political controversies in the 1980s and 1990s over what history is and who owns it were a direct result of these developments.[5] Like the progressive historians of an earlier age, many contemporary historians reject consensus and exceptionalist views of U.S. history and instead present us with a past where conflict and socioeconomic, racial, and gendered divisions and oppressions are not ignored or written out of an imagined past.

The challenge for historians is both to convey and record this broader and more complicated conception of history for larger public audiences and to address the interrogation of the increasingly beleaguered but resilient commitment to "objectivity" and "historical truths" among historians. This is especially true of U.S. history, which has traditionally been characterized by a strong empiricist tradition and an aversion to theory. The decline of the ideal of objectivity in other disciplines, even in the natural sciences after Thomas Kuhn, who showed how revolutions in scientific knowledge were influenced partly by social and historical factors, was paralleled in history.[6] Some historians became more concerned with the world as lived and perceived rather than as explained. The search for a "usable past" led some historians overtly to champion writing history from a subjective rather than an objective perspective. On the other hand, the new quantitative history threatened to reinvent history as a highly empirical and esoteric social science, when the art of narrative remains one of the best ways through which historians can connect with a broader reading public.

One could point out that historians more than any other group of scholars have long been aware of the contingent nature of their interpretations, at least since E. H. Carr argued in *What Is History?* that historical facts do not exist independent of historians' interpretations.[7] At the same time, despite the postmodern turn in theory, most historians have been reluctant to throw the proverbial baby out with the bathwater. Rather than give up on the notion of objectivity completely, historians have become more aware of the constructed nature of objectivity. In this sense, they differ from some of the other humanities where relativism reigns virtually supreme.[8] In other words, most historians would agree that there is no such thing as a "perspectiveless" interpretation but, still, would assert that all interpretations must rest on identified sources. The very nature of historical research—digging into archives or questioning their silences, defining projects particularly by time and space—makes most historians wary of generalizations based on little evidence. The best sort of history, of course, does not lose sight of the particular but at the same time posits broader analytic and causal frameworks, because the purpose of history is not merely to report but to explain. Perhaps it is this understanding of their task that makes many historians skeptical of postmodern theory. It would be a mistake, however, to confuse criticism of postmodernism with a general aversion to theory. This is especially significant in view of the tendency of some conservative critics of the new American history to lump the Left, the new social histories, and postmodernism into one undifferentiated mass.

To view the emergence of the new American histories as merely political is also a mistake. There were some purely academic influences at work: for instance, the French Annalistes and their somewhat naïve obsession with social scientific method and jargon. If anything, the latter trend was conservative rather than radical in its political import. One could also argue that the writing of history has always been a political act. The fact that traditional historians left out large chunks of society from their narrowly conceived accounts of history and at times reduced history to a filiopietistic, national mythology hardly makes those narratives more objective or apolitical.

The controversy over political correctness and heated debates over public history are potent because conservatives still see history's primary task as building a positive national identity and bemoan any emphasis on groups that have been historically exploited. Identity politics and political correctness are not the sole preserve of the Left, as its detractors like to argue. Ironically, the only defense that history as a discipline might mount against this sort of sordid politicization (a good example was the unnecessary controversy over the *Enola Gay* exhibition at the Smithsonian) is to fall back on some agreed upon notion of objectivity.[9] It is hardly surprising that today we can witness a politically motivated attack on a body like the National Endowment for the Humanities, which supports scholars and historians of all stripes. It is not just the kind of history that is being written and disseminated that is under attack; also at risk is the very willingness to accept historical facts or to consider the latest insights on our diverse past that the field has to offer.

While eschewing this sort of rather anti-intellectual and political caviling, one could still raise some valid concerns about the direction of contemporary historical writing in the U.S. Even as historians have broadened their purview in terms of their subject matter, they have narrowed their vision. Increasing specialization in subfields has resulted in the rigid compartmentalization of history into social, economic, political, intellectual, legal, environmental, and cultural categories, to name a prominent few, and its fragmentation into distinct and separate histories of various groups. The need for a historical synthesis, which would incorporate the strengths and avoid the divisions of the new histories, is increasingly evident.[10] Such a synthesis would of course not mean a return to the grand old, exclusionary narrative of American history. A new historical synthesis would instead build on the scholarship of the new histories.

Connected to the absence of a new synthesis of American history is a growing concern with the depoliticization of history, or what was once called the political crisis of social history. The dominance of social history in the past few decades has meant not just the eclipse of traditional political history but also at times evasion of political questions as a whole. Some social historians have produced romanticized and isolated histories of ordinary folk, a sort of pots-and-pans history more concerned with the minutiae of daily life than with questions of power and class relations. As Hobsbawm once noted, historians should be writing a history of society rather than social history.[11] The new political history, with its emphasis on voting records and the ethnic, cultural, and religious loyalties of voters and its reliance on political science methods, has also contributed to a particularly limited view of politics in U.S. history.

Uncritical borrowing of reified, static, and ahistorical social science models has also exacted a heavy toll on the writing of history. The vogue of social science methodology and concepts led to the decline of narrative in history and the art of writing history more generally. Social scientific perspectives might have broadened the scope and content of history, but they have also produced a slew of dull, technical, jargonistic, and unreadable monographs that rarely appeal to broader audiences, leading to a gap between popular historical narratives and fictions written by independent scholars and monographs produced by academic historians. As public history has emerged as a field, it has sought to lessen this gap by creating alternative means of disseminating historical knowledge, particularly through museum exhibitions and digital platforms.[12]

But perhaps it is time that academic historians also pay more attention to narrative and reassert the status of history as a humanities subject, one that pays as much attention to literary style as social scientific method. Concern over the loss of narrative in history is also linked with the view that history should be accessible to a reading public and should play an important role in defining our public culture. In fact, historians, whether academic, public, or independent scholars, have a responsibility not to leave the understanding and memorializing of significant events, such as the sesquicentennial of the Civil War and emancipation, to popularizers and antiquarians who may blur the line between fact and fiction.[13] Some college- or university-based historians are still divided on the role and place of history in the popular imagination and hesitate to try and convey their work to larger audiences. The recent popularity of historical films and books about slavery and race reveals that there is a public appetite for history, which historians should not hesitate to satisfy.[14]

Unlike other social scientists, historians have also strangely neglected to carve out a role for themselves on issues of public policy. Indeed, a historian's viewpoint is sorely needed in current debates over immigration and constitutional and civil liberties. But most historians are wary of merely writing "presentist" and relevant histories or conforming to the idea of a usable past, which might undermine or threaten the integrity of their scholarship. This is not, however, a zero-sum game. It is perfectly possible for us to adhere to our disciplinary standards of evidence and argument and to use our scholarship to make important interventions in the public world. The contributions of historians like C. Vann Woodward, for instance, on behalf of desegregation during the Civil Rights movement are instructive. In short, American historians should be willing to address the age-old question of the relationship between theory and practice, something that social scientists do on a daily basis.

The contribution of the new histories has not been so much to banish old histories or traditional areas of study like political history but to give us a broader, more complex, and more nuanced view of American history.[15] The redefinition of what constitutes the historical, a revolution in historical method and scope, attempts to write historical narratives for a broader lay public, and public interest in the history of ordinary Americans, as evidenced by the interest in such purveyors of history to the wider public as the tenement museum in New York City and the Smithsonian's National Museum of African American History and Culture—all of these bode well for the future of the historical profession and public history. Many history graduates are opting for careers in museums, archives, libraries, publishing houses, and public history sites rather than in academics. Before the social history revolution, that was hardly the case. As long as popularization does not compromise the standards that define the discipline, such as facts and analysis, and popular interest in history does not diminish, there should be room for optimism for the future of the production and dissemination of historical knowledge.

1   R. G. Collingwood, *The Idea of History* (Oxford, 1946); Fritz Stern, ed., *The Varieties of History: From Voltaire to the Present* (New York, 1973); G. W. F. Hegel, *The Philosophy of History*, trans. J. Silbree (New York, 1900).

2   Gary Nash, Charlotte Crabtree, and Ross Dunn, *History on Trial: Culture Wars and the Teaching of the Past* (New York, 1997); Lynn Cheney quoted in Sean Wilentz, "Don't Know Much About History," *New York Times*, Nov. 30, 1997.

3   James A. Henretta, "Social History as Lived and Written," *American Historical Review* 84(1979):1293–1322.

4   Sadie Bergen, "Getting Warmer: Historians on Climate Change and the Anthropocene," *Perspectives on History* 55(2017):7–8.

5   Dipesh Chakrabarty, *Provincializing Europe: Postcolonial Thought and Historical Difference* (Princeton, 2000); Eric Foner, *Who Owns History? Rethinking the Past in a Changing World* (New York, 2002).

6 Thomas S. Kuhn, *The Structure of Scientific Revolutions* (Chicago, 1962).

7 E. H. Carr, *What Is History?* (New York, 1962).

8 Peter Novick, *That Noble Dream: The "Objectivity Question" and the American Historical Profession* (Cambridge, 1988); Joyce Appleby, Lynn Hunt, and Margaret Jacob, *Telling the Truth About History* (New York, 1994).

9 "History and the Public: What Can We Handle? A Round Table About History after the *Enola Gay* Controversy," *Journal of American History* 82(1995):1085–1093.

10 Thomas Bender, "Wholes and Parts: The Need for Synthesis in American History," *Journal of American History* 73(1986):120–136.

11 Eric J. Hobsbawm, "From Social History to the History of Society," *Daedalus* 100(1971):20–45.

12 Kristin Nowratzki and Jack Dougherty, eds., *Writing History in the Digital Age* (Ann Arbor, 2013).

13 David Samuels, "The Call of Stories," *Lingua Franca* 5(May/June 1995):35–43.

14 Manisha Sinha, "Slavery in Cinema," *Dissent* (Spring 2017):16–20.

15 Frederik Logevall and Kenneth Osgood, "Why Did We Stop Teaching Political History?," *New York Times*, Aug. 29, 2016.

John Lauritz Larson

The Feedback Loop: Sharing the Process of Telling Stories

HISTORY IS NOT an objective commodity, possessed and preserved by an academic priesthood and presented to an ignorant but adoring congregation. History is a complex, negotiated settlement constructed by a multitude of actors—participants, witnesses, pundits, propagandists, scholars, curators, and amateur buffs, drawn from every race, gender, and station. It is a process by which we craft the stories of our shared lives. We use it to anchor our collective identities, to affirm authentic experiences, and to impose some sense of narrative coherence on the otherwise random facts of life lived in real time. It is a never-ending project, and it results in many stories, each of which, in some way, is true and important.

The existence of multiple truths has challenged historians time and again—notably in the 1960s with "bottom-up" social history and again in the 1990s when linguists and cultural critics called into question all sorts of narrative and analysis. If a priesthood controls interpretation and can license or "ordain" its acolytes, it can hope to retain control and damp down (or torch?) heretical voices, but in an open society with ever more streams of information and explanation avail-

John Lauritz Larson teaches history at Purdue University. While his scholarship has focused on American economic development in the eighteenth and nineteenth centuries, his teaching has kept him engaged broadly with hundreds of entry-level undergraduates as well as the general public. He currently is finishing a book about American freedom, progress, and environmental impact from Sir Walter Raleigh to Teddy Roosevelt, tentatively entitled "Laid Waste."

able to all kinds of people, such authority is a mirage. The high priests of academic history can learn to meet with the people to negotiate common ground, or they can watch them walk out the door, never to return. The feedback loop between historian and audience is not just a comment card or a student evaluation; it is a constitutive function of the process of doing history in the postmodern twenty-first century.

This insight did not come to me easily or quickly. (In fact, the illusion of control was only dashed, finally, by having two teenagers in the house.) But after almost two decades of trying to dispense knowledge like a pharmacist dispenses pills, I began to look more seriously into the role of the feedback loop. What do my students *want* to know? And why do they want to know it? The question put me in mind of an episode early in my career when I came face to face with the limitations of presumed expertise.

I started my career at an outdoor "living history" museum dedicated to portraying pioneer life in Indiana in the year 1836. I had just finished graduate school and was eager to share what I knew (or thought I knew) as a result of my shiny new education. One day, I encountered a young mother in one of our 1836 period cabins, who proclaimed to her children that this homestead was "just like" the one that her grandfather had grown up in. Since her grandfather likely grew up in the 1930s, not the 1830s, I rushed to correct the error and enlighten her children about the *real* pioneers, as well as the ignorance of their mother. Imagine my surprise when my expertise was greeted with a cold huff and an abrupt departure. This was my first encounter with the feedback loop. That woman had opened the negotiation with something she thought she recognized. She had thrown me a line with which I might have pulled myself into the space between what she "knew" and what I was hoping to explain to her. But I threw her a stone, and our educational moment promptly sank.

Fast forward eighteen years. In the late 1990s, I asked two large sections of my history survey class at Purdue to answer some reckless questions. "What was on your mind when you first woke up this morning?" I asked one class. "What do you worry about most?" I asked another. I got over two hundred responses altogether, and after grouping them rather coarsely, I found that the answers fell into four topical categories: race, money, sex, and salvation. That is to say, my twenty-something students were interested, overwhelmingly, in making a living, finding a mate, achieving some form of racial and social harmony, and getting right with God however they envisioned Him.

Here were things about which *history* has something to say! These exact challenges probably bothered Elizabethan Englishmen and Powhatan Indians alike. They might even serve as the bedrock on which I could construct historical stories that honored change over time *and* resonated with the timeless issues that loomed in the minds of modern students. Who am I? And who are these strangers? How will I sustain myself? What can I do with this relentless sexual urge? What happens when I die? Young adults are hardwired to look to the future. How could I get them to look to the past for guidance and inspiration?

I began to imagine the passage of time as a musical score. Intricate melodies and harmonies dance around the upper reaches of the staff. Soprano and midrange voices sing of what is special and unique about each time and place history claims to record. But at the bottom of the register lies the "continuo," a line of bass notes and rhythms that persist, verse after verse, linking transient melodic figures to the persistent realities of birth and death, youth and age, poverty and wealth, slavery and freedom, hope and despair that mark the human experience in every time and place. Scholars with professional credentials may know a great deal about the soprano and alto lines, but every living human being knows in her or his bones the base—the bass—realities of life lived. There's a moment in John Steinbeck's *Grapes of Wrath* when the California-bound Joads meet a family that is actually *returning*, busted, from the Golden Shore. "S'pose he's tellin' the truth—that fella?" Pa said about the discouraging tale he had just heard. "He's tellin' the truth, awright," answered Casy. "The truth for him. He wasn't makin' nothin' up." "How about us?" asked young Tom Joad. "Is that the truth for us?" "I don' know," said the preacher.[1]

Just in time for a new century, I embarked on a radical overhaul of the U.S. history survey from Columbus to Reconstruction. I now approach the class in three units: two period murals—the colonial world and the antebellum world—separated by a Revolutionary experience that I approach in a conventional narrative as a transformative interlude. In the colonial and antebellum units, I spend one week each on the four themes of race, money, sex, and salvation. Like different tracks of a recording, I lay them down horizontally and ask the students to look for vertical connections as the complexities emerge. At first, nobody knows what to expect, but they give me the benefit of the doubt for a couple of weeks—long enough for me to lay out a few examples and begin to capture their interest.

Nothing in their past experience has prepared students to approach history this way. Everything has taught them to look for names, dates, chronology, and famous people and events. Instead, I approach my themes like an anthropologist trying to understand a people just discovered in some wilderness (which, of course, is exactly what occurred in the Americas between 1492 and 1650). The agonizing fear and excitement that must have gripped the 104 men and boys who landed at Jamestown naturally create a dramatic moment, echoes of which young people fresh from the homes of their childhood cannot fail to recognize. I begin building the problems of race relations out of the Englishmen's bewildering encounters with indigenous "others," experiences marked by fear and terrible anxiety as much as fixed conviction. I introduce African slavery in a similar way—as a solution to a labor problem that itself sprang from a tobacco boom fueled by desperate colonists trying to scratch out a living (or seize a fortune) before death caught up with them.

By focusing on my four themes throughout the colonial story, I manage to emphasize not the role of heroic persons in an untouchable past, but rather the questions of "how the world works" that confronted ordinary men and women, young and old. Key events—the founding of colonies, wars and violent outbreaks, political crises, even revolutions back in England—all make their appearance, but they are framed by the single ambition of understanding how it might have looked to people "like me" caught up in that time and place. As a result, the interactions between men and women, masters and servants, and the rich and the poor, as well as among the Natives, invading settlers, and their African captives, lie exposed where students of various backgrounds and interests can find a point of connection with their own quest to know how the world works for them.

My objective as the instructor is to show them the past as a resource on which they can draw once they are armed with a few simple tools of enquiry and interpretation. This limited ambition doubtless grows out of my experience teaching thousands of undergraduates whose majors are in science, technology, engineering, and agriculture. I am not preparing future graduate students—in fact, I make it a point to assure them this approach is meant to offer a general "app" for living. To prove that I am not kidding, in advance of their exams I give them the questions, for which they can readily find the "stuff" in their notes, readings, and lectures, but they must arrange such stuff in order to answer the questions effectively. (Oddly enough, a surprising number of students at my public university blow off the first of these exams by not even bothering to distinguish Bacon's Rebellion from Bacon's theory of scientific enquiry. Fewer do so the second time around.)

Having set up a picture of the colonial experience in four parallel registers, I introduce the Revolution with one simple question: Why did these people suddenly feel compelled to leave the empire? Leading actors in that story told us at staggering length what was on their minds after 1765, but some of what they claimed does not match the experiences we discussed in unit one. The central dynamic of this narrative interlude turns on four points. Who wanted a revolution? Who did not? How did they go about trying to recruit people to either position? Why on earth would *you* choose to take up arms for such a cause? One extremely useful resource has been *My Brother Sam Is Dead*, a Newberry Award–winning novel by James Lincoln Collier and Christopher Collier, which frames the problem in just this way.

By treating the Revolution as a hotly contested enterprise, I am then able to introduce the evidence of conflict and variability in the experiences of war, survival, institution building, and governance at the local, state, and federal levels. The outcome remains in doubt right through the Constitution, the Federalist era, and the election of Thomas Jefferson. The central scriptures of the Founding—the

Declaration of Independence and the Constitution of 1787—become instrumental gambits, negotiations by the actors themselves in behalf of objectives never shared entirely by "the people." The American Founding comes out of this unit as a work in progress, not a *fait accompli*, which makes approaching the chaos of the early nineteenth century infinitely easier.

The antebellum unit begins with the question, what do liberty and equality mean to you? So many possible answers, so little time! With irony you can taste, we discover that liberty for ordinary white Americans resulted in a hardening of racial consciousness—in a "final solution" for Natives called "Indian Removal" and in a cotton revolution that stopped the first antislavery impulse dead in its tracks. We find that republican self-government expanded (white male) citizen participation in politics in such a way as to redefine the roles of statesmen and electors. Ideally, a republic rested on citizens who shared common interests and ambitions, but in practice competing interests morphed into the dreaded "factions" that could ruin any form of republican government. Democratization and mobility in the face of pluralistic values and experiences undermined institutions of social consensus and control—the class structure, the family, and the churches.

Meanwhile, the expansion of freedom to pursue innovation and exploit economic opportunities fostered a market revolution that produced marked *dependency* for an ever-increasing number of wage-earning workers. One man's freedom resulted in another people's servitude in a new liberal market for labor. The promise of freedom and independence stood contradicted by the convergence of unanticipated consequences, such as rising inequality, declining autonomy, and arbitrary market forces (such as panics) that crushed the welfare of many workers, farmers, and businessmen. At the personal level, the triumphant "age of Jackson" often proved to be an age of profound anxiety, loss, and frustration.

Having exposed the variety of consequences arising from Revolutionary liberation, I turn finally to the various reform movements and voluntary associations with which Americans in the early republic tried to damp down the chaos and reinforce good order. Irreligion, alcohol abuse, domestic violence, mental illness, prisons, orphanages, schools, and asylums all came in for scrutiny and "correction," mostly through extra-governmental initiatives made necessary by the inability of democratic politics to impose behavioral standards on a free people. In the midst of these campaigns, women activists took up their own cause, demanding civil rights. Many of these women migrated steadily into abolition, joining a legion of free blacks in an attack on the culture of compromise (don't ask, don't tell) that disabled the hand of the nation-state on the morally vexing issue of slavery.

I make it a point to credit the claims of both sides, North and South, as we descend into Civil War: history could, did, and must support both sets of stories, because each was true in its time and place, doing work its supporters needed and wanted done. Although I make it clear in an editorial voice that I support emancipation and equal rights, I make it equally clear that in 1863 many (perhaps most) Americans did *not*, that emancipation gave African Americans "nothing but freedom," and that the state of Indiana did not remove the "black exclusion" clause from its constitution until 1881. As the course ends, there remains on the agenda for the late nineteenth and twentieth centuries race relations without slavery, economic degradation and wealth inequality, gender inequality and sexual regulation, and the roles of church and state in fostering salvation. The "continuo" line persists.

The feedback I get from this approach to the early American survey generally is not about the conclusions I suggest or the answers students glean from the material presented. The feedback mostly references the novelty of the method and the challenge it raises by including the active curiosity of the students themselves in the process of understanding history. I urge them constantly to "connect the dots," but they seldom wind up connecting the dots in the same way because, at bottom, history is a negotiated settlement in which they have an interest and play a constitutive part. My great hope is that they learn that if they can read and write and think, they possess the basic skills with which to engage the historical record on their own.

They can find the factual dots and see what connections are possible. They can challenge the dishonest historical claims with which we are bombarded every day. They can protect themselves from a culture awash in fraud.

History's so-called "master narrative" might be true in one register yet profoundly irrelevant in another. Our own personal histories may stand at odds with some or even most of the textbook version. The dissonance does not invalidate either. The dissonance should challenge us to come to the treaty ground and look for ways to fit the clashing truths together. In his farewell address in January 2017, President Obama asserted correctly that race relations in America have improved dramatically in the past fifty years. "But we're not where we need to be," he added. For people born in the twenty-first century, who were not in the storm of the 1950s and '60s, the recent string of un-punished killings of young black men by police and vigilantes surely supports a different conclusion. Both claims are true and yet starkly contradictory. The feedback loop reminds us that we rarely see the whole picture.

Such conundrums—true facts that contradict each other—persist whenever we acknowledge the different registers and multiple perspectives that constitute history. A resolution to such contradictions continues to elude me, but the problem looms large in the future of history. As we embrace the feedback loop and a multiplicity of narratives, we risk unleashing a rhetorical free-for-all in which unsubstantiated claims and outright falsehoods compete successfully with legitimate, differing perspectives. Students of history, practitioners of all sorts, will need to pay special attention to the structures of logic and documentation that link evidence with valid arguments. This will not be accomplished by reference to degrees, credentials, or publication records; it will have to be addressed in plain, accessible language right alongside our historical claims themselves.

I once feared that the contradictions in historical narratives showed a failure to understand. Further research, surely, would unearth the point of reconciliation. Now I wonder if the contradictions don't spring from the very nature of our existence. Total coherence was an illusion, made possible only by squelching dissonant channels in order to boost one dominant stream of memory and explanation. Perhaps we must be satisfied with a disciplined process and a negotiated settlement. "S'pose he's tellin' the truth—that fella?" Pa said about the discouraging tale he had just heard. "He's tellin' the truth, awright," answered Casy. "The truth for him. He wasn't makin' nothin' up." "How about us?" asked young Tom Joad. "Is that the truth for us?" "I don' know," said the preacher.

1 John Steinbeck, *The Grapes of Wrath*, ed. Robert DeMott (1939; New York, 2006), 191.

Robert Townsend

Academic History's Challenges and Opportunities

THE HISTORY PROFESSION in academia finds itself beset by difficulties in 2017. For faculty members seeing a growing number of empty seats in their classes, as well as doctoral students and their advisers looking out at future career prospects within the academy, this is a difficult time. History course enrollments and majors have declined sharply in recent years, and the opportunities for new doctoral students appear to be falling along with them.

Regrettably, the immediate problems for academic history will be difficult to turn around in the short term, as they represent the convergence of large structural and cultural challenges that transcend the discipline. Nevertheless, as a profession, academic history needs to look to the past for reference points and potential guidance out of this impasse and set its sights on a better future. The discipline has been in similar situations in the past and recovered. Too often, however, it failed to learn from those difficult experiences and fell back into complacency and bad habits that led to another crisis. The profession needs to learn from past mistakes, both to find a way out of its cur-

Robert Townsend oversees the Washington office of the American Academy of Arts and Sciences and day-to-day work on the Humanities Indicators project. Prior to the Academy, he spent twenty-four years at the American Historical Association in positions ranging from Editorial Assistant to Deputy Director. He is the author of *History's Babel* (2013) and the author or co-author of over two hundred articles on various aspects of history, higher education, and electronic publishing.

rent difficulties and to institutionalize practices that will prevent—or at least ameliorate—the next ebb tide.

CHASING STUDENTS

The first, and perhaps largest, challenge for the history profession in academia is the rapid decline in the number of students taking classes and going on to major in the subject. In a survey by the American Historical Association (AHA) in 2016, more than half of history departments reported their enrollments had declined over 10 percent in just three years.[1]

Alongside falling enrollments, the trends in the number of college majors appeared equally dire; the number of college majors fell by 20 percent from 2012 to 2015 (the most recent year with data). And in terms of "market share" for history degrees, the situation looks somewhat worse. As a percentage of all bachelor's degrees conferred, history degrees started falling in the 2007 academic year, when history accounted for 2.3 percent of all baccalaureate degrees awarded. As of 2015, the discipline was conferring less than 1.6 percent of all bachelor's degrees—a historic low in records that extend back to 1949.[2]

While the trends are clear and alarming, the reasons for the declines are a bit less tangible. One common explanation is a cultural shift against the humanities at large, a turn that questions the economic value of a degree in the field and the career prospects of graduates. For those who follow media accounts on these subjects, it is easy to find articles arguing both sides of this case—often framed as an argument with recalcitrant parents who would prevent their children from majoring in a humanities subject. And the situation is not improved when even a friendly president tells students, "I promise you folks can make a lot more, potentially, with skilled manufacturing or the trades than they might with an art history degree." History is not alone in this challenge, as the number of graduates has been falling in almost every humanities discipline in recent years. Similar to the other disciplines in the field, history appears to be struggling to respond to these financial pressures, particularly relative to the obvious career paths for vocational subjects, or the higher salaries offered in some of the science, technology, engineering, and medicine (STEM) fields. As a result, students and parents are increasingly questioning the "return on investment" for a humanities degree, and policy makers have started to propose policies that would actively encourage students to shift their majors to disciplines that serve preferred economic interests.[3]

The cultural explanation seems partial and insufficient, however, as the discipline faces other structural challenges in attracting students. As of 2015, an unprecedented number of students were taking and passing Advanced Placement (AP) history tests, which allowed them to avoid taking an introductory history course at the four-year college level. At the same time, ever-larger numbers of students are bypassing introductory history courses at the four-year college level by earning credits through dual enrollment high school classes and community college classes. These trends have been building over two decades, but the numbers are staggering: almost nine hundred thousand students took AP history examinations in 2015, and more than half earned a passing score.[4]

For history faculty at community colleges, these trends are proving something of a boon, as an unprecedented number of students are earning two-year liberal arts and liberal studies degrees (which generally include history as a core requirement). For faculty members in history departments at four-year colleges and universities, however, the same dynamic has made it increasingly difficult to make that initial connection with students that often takes place in an introductory class. There are many well-intentioned reasons for these changes—reducing costs to students and helping them finish their degrees expeditiously—but they are having a clear and deleterious effect on enrollments and majors at the four-year college level. Without the opportunity to make an initial contact with students in the classroom and the chance to encourage the best students to continue on and major in the subject, history departments will find it increasingly difficult to attract students.

The current declines in history enrollments and majors echo a challenging period for history departments in the 1970s. From 1971 to 1984, the number of students graduating with bachelor's degrees in history fell 63 percent (from 44,931 to 16,546). Contemporaneous accounts from the period cited a sharp increase in the number of colleges and universities dropping history from the general education requirements at their institutions, and other similar-sounding accounts voiced rising doubts about the economic value of a history degree. What the history discipline faces today seems comparable, even though history has been restored to the general education requirements (which led to sharp increases in the number of history majors in the 1990s and 2000s). The difference today is that students are finding new ways around those requirements, but the outcome is the same. Students who never set foot in an introductory history classroom are considerably less likely to go on to major in the discipline.[5]

One of the other great challenges for the profession in academia lies in a shift in the reading habits of the general public, and the profession's limited ability to adjust to these changes. There is a growing body of evidence that shows waning interest in long-form reading among the U.S. population. According to the Pew Research Center, in 2016 one out of five Americans had not read a single book in the previous year, and the median annual number of books (in any subject) read by Americans aged eighteen to twenty-nine was just five. Data from the federal government also shows that the amount of time spent reading for pleasure has also been falling. On average, Americans spent twenty-one minutes a day reading for pleasure in 2015—a decline of six minutes in just a decade. Meanwhile, time spent on computers for entertainment grew to surpass reading, and both were dwarfed by the amount of time spent watching television.[6]

These trends suggest a deep challenge for a discipline that remains heavily focused on creating and teaching print books, and some departments have responded to declining enrollments by curtailing their reading requirements. During the Future of History workshop for which this volume is named, there was considerable discussion (and skepticism) about the merits of the standard method of teaching the introductory course. For good or ill, there is little evidence of a change in the way college and university faculty are teaching their students, particularly in lower-level courses. A survey of history faculty in colleges and universities found relatively few taking up new teaching methods in 2015. Indeed, almost 90 percent of the faculty members surveyed reported that they "always" or "often" used the lecture format for their undergraduate courses. While almost all of them reported using presentation software, such as PowerPoint, the evidence suggests traditional methods continue to prevail. A handful of the respondents to the survey stoutly defended the lecture course as still the best vehicle for conveying content knowledge, but most were silent on why this method seemed preferable.[7]

Perhaps the underlying influence here, the one that is not getting the attention it needs, is the preparation of new faculty for the history classroom. There is little evidence of substantial improvements in the way doctoral students in history are prepared for their professional work as classroom teachers. In a 2012 survey, less than one in four history departments at a research university reported offering a seminar focused on digital methods for research and teaching. The discipline has a long history of neglecting this aspect of its professional preparation, and there is little evidence that has changed. This haphazard approach to sending faculty into the history classroom merely exacerbates the larger challenges for the discipline.[8]

CHASING JOBS

The future health of the profession within the academy is not just a matter of current training practices, as the decline in the number of students taking history courses presents a tangible threat to the future vitality of the discipline. Alongside the economic challenge that declining student enrollments and majors pose for history departments at four-year colleges and universities, the drop-off in students has contributed to a greatly constricted job market for new PhDs. As an area of employment, history has rarely seemed so beleaguered. As of the 2015 academic year, the number of new PhDs being conferred was near historically high levels, while the number of job openings lingered near historic lows (in records that extend back to the early 1970s).[9]

The current trends mark a striking reversal in a very short period of time. Nine years ago, colleges and universities were advertising an unprecedented number of jobs, with more than 1,000 positions advertised with the AHA in each academic year from 2006 to 2008. During the recession, the number of jobs fell below 600 openings in two years, recovered slightly, and then fell back below 600 positions in the most recent academic year (2016). While academic job opportunities were falling, the number of history PhDs awarded each year continued to grow—rising from 971 doctorates conferred in 2008 to 1,182 in 2014 (before falling slightly the following year).[10]

Although the widening gap between academic jobs and PhDs may appear irrational, it is important to keep in mind that it takes an average of eight years to finish a history PhD. As a result, most of the students finishing degrees today started when the job market appeared rich with opportunity. And even after the job market began to fall, most doctoral programs were slow to cut back on new admissions. According to information submitted to the AHA, the average number of students applying to doctoral programs continued to increase until 2011—in part due to opportunities and financial incentives for those un- or under-employed during the recession. Given the scale of the recession at the time, many doctoral programs clung to the hope that the drop in jobs was just a temporary reflection of the larger economic crisis, and many continued to admit students at the same rate as in the pre-recession years. As a result, the number of doctoral students in history programs continued to rise until about 2011. It is only in recent years that admissions and enrollments in doctoral programs have started to fall, though that still leaves a large number of doctoral students stepping into a very difficult academic job market.[11]

Improvements that could address the problem run up against large structural challenges that shape the academic job market. Growing student enrollments and majors helped many departments add tenure-track positions from the late 1980s up to 2008. The subsequent declines have made it increasingly difficult for departments to replace departing faculty, much less make the case to add new members to the department.[12]

The shrinking number of undergraduate students presents only one of the problems for those looking to enter employment in academia.

Adding to the challenge for those seeking an academic job is a demographic valley in the number of history faculty members approaching retirement. Consider that in 1995 almost 40 percent of the faculty would reach peak retirement years within the following decade—a decade that coincided with an unprecedented run-up in the number of job openings. As of 2015, however, the share of history faculty approaching retirement had fallen to just 22 percent, with an unusually large demographic bubble of history faculty at the associate professor rank. The evidence suggests that even if the problem of student enrollments turned around tomorrow, relatively few job openings would arise from faculty retirements.[13]

Here, again, the problems in history are reflected across most of the humanities disciplines, as every large disciplinary society in the field has reported declines of 30 percent or more in advertised jobs. As a result, a growing number of organizations, including the AHA, the National Endowment for the Humanities, and the Andrew W. Mellon Foundation, are actively promoting "career diversity" for PhDs. Similar to the moves of some programs at the undergraduate level, these organizations are trying to promote greater transparency about the job prospects for doctoral students and describe more explicitly the range of skills students acquire in the course of their studies. Unlike the efforts for undergraduates, however, departments are working proactively to create (or at least light the way to) new employment pathways for their doctoral degree recipients.[14]

These programs to promote and support career diversity are not unprecedented. During a similar job crisis in the 1970s, doctoral programs and the AHA also explored ways to open up career opportunities for history PhDs outside of academia. While that undertaking helped fuel the development of the public history movement in the late 1970s, much of the energy behind such efforts within PhD programs faded in the 1980s as the annual number of new history PhDs fell into alignment with the available number of jobs. Similar initiatives during a milder job crisis in the mid to late 1990s also evaporated during the substantial burst in jobs in the early 2000s. If the past is any guide to the future, it remains an open question whether the current efforts will prove equally evanescent. When PhDs fall into alignment with job openings or jobs rise again to match the number of PhDs, it remains to be seen whether PhD programs have put in place lasting structural changes that prepare the discipline for the next job crisis.[15]

MAKING A BETTER CASE FOR HISTORY

The convergence of issues afflicting the academic history profession points to a general challenge for every history department. If the discipline is to recover from the current downturn in its fortunes, it will need to do a better job of making a case for itself. At the undergraduate level, this starts with two critical steps—better outreach to students who would otherwise circumvent history courses in the department and being more proactive in helping students see the value of taking a history course and, ultimately, earning a degree in the discipline.

Across the humanities, a growing number of departments and schools are developing new ways of getting the attention of students and attracting them into their programs. These efforts vary from place to place but include programmatic efforts to reach students in high school classes and community colleges, introductory seminars for first-year students that demonstrate some of the skills and habits of mind they could develop in coursework, and creative minors and second majors specifically intended to draw in students from other fields (such as the Viking studies minor at Cornell and the establishment of medical- and business-humanities programs at several schools).[16]

Once departments draw students into a class, a growing number are also working to make the potential advantages of historical study more transparent. Departments at public universities seem especially active on this front, encouraging faculty members to state clearly the skills that students will acquire in the course of their classes and to articulate the tangible life benefits students can gain from their studies. The former comprises many process skills with broad application, such as the ability to do research, to assemble evidence, and to write well; the latter encompasses the particular cognitive developments that improve with/arise from historical study, such as critical thinking and the ability to place things in historical context. The AHA's recent Tuning project reflects a discipline-wide push to articulate these values and provide easy-to-adapt tools that will help departments do so.[17] The key here lies in the effort to ensure that no student enters a history classroom without a clear sense that they will finish with more than just a body of content knowledge—they will be leaving with a set of tangible skills that will serve them throughout their lives.

Alongside the need to reach out and make the case for the value of each class, history departments can also point to evidence of the long-term value of a history major. There is ample evidence to show that students who graduate with degrees in history enjoy relatively low levels of unemployment and relatively high average earnings (and not only in comparison to other humanities disciplines). In 2013, for instance, the median earnings of students who had majored in U.S. history were above the average for graduates from almost every other field. (The exceptions were engineering and the physical sciences.) Faculty members and administrators in history departments should familiarize themselves with the data and arm their students with the necessary information for those occasions when family members (and even presidents) may question the return on investment of a history major.[18]

In addition to creating the opportunities and tools needed to make the case to students, the history profession should take advantage of the emerging cultural environment for history. The view from Washington suggests that the recent elections may provide an important opportunity to shift the conversation from the narrow economic benefits of history studies to the potential excitement of intellectual engagement in a transformative moment. Since November 8, there has been an explosion of writing and editorials positioning the election in a historical perspective and using current events as an opportunity to rearticulate the value of those insights to society. The ongoing contests over antecedents for the issues of the moment extend from the Founding of the nation to the Civil Rights era within U.S. history, draw on historical parallels from around the world, and examine the preceding decades and centuries of flows of peoples into the nation and around the globe. These discussions appear to create an opening for the discipline, though it remains to be seen whether historians can connect to this rising interest and leverage these discussions to increase numbers of students, as similar debates did during the 1960s. Here, again, it will require proactive efforts on the part of faculty members to reach potential students and make the case.

If past experience serves as a precedent, the recent decline in undergraduate enrollments, majors, and faculty jobs will stabilize and ultimately reverse to some degree. The question that remains is how far they will fall before they reach a new equilibrium. Will the number of history majors fall by more than 50 percent again, as in the 1970s, before the discipline partially recovers? And what will be the effect on the future health of the discipline if the number of new PhDs falls by half before the next wave of retirements begins anew?

To some extent, the fate of the history discipline is tied to forces beyond its control. If well-meaning politicians and academic leaders continue to build paths around history classrooms, faculty will find themselves chasing students dispersed ever further out of their reach. Ultimately, it falls to every member of a history department to view their contacts with every student as an opportunity to sell the discipline and help create a better future for the past.

1 Julia Brookins, "Survey Finds Fewer Students Enrolling in College History Courses," *Perspectives on History: The Newsmagazine of the American Historical Association*, Sept. 2016. *Perspectives* is available online via the website of the American Historical Association, www.historians.org.

2 "Bachelor's Degrees in the Humanities," *Humanities Indicators*, March 2016. *Humanities Indicators* is available online at www.humanitiesindicators.org.

3 Scott Jaschik, "Apology from Obama," *Inside Higher Ed*, Feb. 19, 2014, www.insidehighered.com; Steven Pearlstein, "Meet the Parents Who Won't Let Their Children Study Literature," *Washington Post*, Sept. 2, 2016.

4 "Advanced Placement Exams Taken in the Humanities," *Humanities Indicators*, Sept. 2016.

5 "History Degree Completions," *Humanities Indicators*, April 2016. On the importance of the introductory course in the selection of a college major, see Daniel

F. Chambliss and Christopher G. Takacs, *How College Works* (Cambridge, Mass., 2014), 50–61.

6 Andrew Perrin, "Book Reading 2016," Sept. 1, 2016, Pew Research Center, www .pewinternet.org/2016/09/01/book-reading-2016/; "Time Spent Reading," *Humanities Indicators*, Sept. 2016.

7 Robert B. Townsend, "Teaching Practices and Technology in History," *Perspectives on History* (forthcoming).

8 Susan White, Raymond Chu, and Roman Czujko, *The 2012–13 Survey of Humanities Departments at Four-Year Institutions* (College Park, Md., 2014; sponsored by the American Academy of Arts and Sciences), 99.

9 Robert B. Townsend and Emily Swafford, "Conflicting Signals in the Academic Job Market for History," *Perspectives on History*, Jan. 2017.

10 Townsend and Swafford, "Conflicting Signals in the Academic Job Market."

11 Unpublished data from the American Historical Association's annual survey of history doctoral programs, tabulated by the author.

12 Robert B. Townsend, "The Ecology of the History Job: Shifting Realities in a Fluid Market," *Perspectives on History*, Dec. 2011.

13 Robert B. Townsend and Julia Brookins, "The Troubled Academic Job Market for History" *Perspectives on History*, Feb. 2016.

14 Statistics from "Ongoing Weakness in the Academic Job Market for Humanities," American Academy of Arts and Sciences Data Forum, www.amacad.org. For more on the AHA initiative, see "Career Diversity for Historians," Jobs and Professional Development, www.historians.org. Information on the Andrew W. Mellon Foundation's efforts can be found in Cristle Collins Judd, "Revitalizing Graduate Education," Andrew W. Mellon Foundation, Sept. 20, 2016, www.mellon.org. For the NEH program, see Vimal Patel, "Grants Seek to Foster a Culture Change in Humanities Graduate Education," *Chronicle of Higher Education*, Aug. 9, 2016.

15 Robert B. Townsend, "History in Those Hard Times: Looking for Jobs in the 1970s," *Perspectives on History*, Sept. 2009.

16 For examples of outreach efforts, see Michelle Yiu, "Yale Builds Humanities Outreach Network," *Yale Daily News*, March 4, 2016, and Kathleen J. Sullivan, "Stanford Faculty Launch a New Humanities Core," *Stanford News*, May 10, 2016. See also Anna Carmichael, "New A&S Minors Offer Studies of Vikings, Policy, Capitalism and Prisons," Cornell University College of Arts and Sciences, Sept. 14, 2016, www.as.cornell.edu.

17 For the Tuning project, see Tuning the History Discipline page on the American

Historical Association website: www.historians.org/teaching-and-learning/tuning-the-history-discipline.

18 "Earnings of Humanities Majors with a Terminal Bachelor's Degree," *Humanities Indicators*; Rob Townsend "Where Can You Find Data on Career Prospects for History Majors?" *AHA Today*, Oct. 12, 2015, www.blog.historians.org.

Stephen A. Marini
Reflections on Historical Authority in the Digital Age

ONE

The first time I heard about the impact of the Internet on historical authority was in the early 1990s. I had made the transition to personal computing with my trusty Kaypro II and floppy disks when I received an invitation to attend a conference at Yale on the future of church history. On the weekend program was a Sunday morning session featuring a talk by Prof. Harry S. Stout, one of our faculty hosts, on history and computerization. I was aware that social historians had been analyzing data by computer for some time, but I knew virtually nothing about the World Wide Web and had no idea whatsoever that it might influence my research and teaching in some way.

What Stout said astonished me. He reported that the advent of browsers had transformed the nature of historical research by making information available indiscriminately to anyone able to conduct a simple web search. The problem was that some websites filtered historical information through highly partisan religious or political

Stephen A. Marini is Elisabeth Luce Moore Professor of Christian Studies, Professor of Religion in America and Ethics, and Chair of the Department of Religion at Wellesley College. He is the author of *Radical Sects of Revolutionary New England* (1982) and *Sacred Song in America: Religion, Music, and Public Culture* (2003). He is also founder and singing master of Norumbega Harmony, a choral ensemble specializing in early American psalmody, and general editor of its tunebook, *The Norumbega Harmony: Historic and Contemporary Hymn Tunes and Anthems from the New England Singing School Tradition* (2003).

perspectives, while others posted material responsibly in ways that were independently verifiable. Our colleague reported that he was now receiving papers based on information from the former, in which students were unable to detect the bias of the site and, therefore, had reproduced its assumptions as factual reality.

Stout's prediction for the future of historical work was equally dire. He argued that we cannot expect to control this new flow of information that mixes fact and opinion arbitrarily. It would simply overwhelm any academic effort to resist it. The best we could do was to interrogate the sites ourselves, recommend the most reliable ones to our students, and require them to document which sites they use so that we could check the informational basis of their work. To me, it seemed a Sisyphean task at best. Historians had lost their exclusive access to research data, and their cultural license to interpret history authoritatively was beginning to run out.

Fast forward twenty-five years to a dinner party in a leafy Boston exurb during October 2016, attended by political activists, business leaders, and academics. During a break in the conversation, a senior financial advisor asked us all to address two key questions that had been troubling him: "What is going on with social media, and why don't they teach history in schools anymore?" The company agreed on the urgency of these questions, but no one had good answers to them. A few weeks later, Donald Trump was elected president of the United States after a campaign reliant on false "news" and "postfactual" claims, many of them historical—from conspiracy theories about the Kennedy assassination and the 9/11 attacks to Holocaust denial—fed to millions of American voters through Facebook, Twitter, and highly partisan online news sites. Those ruminations from that long-ago Yale conference had proved prophetic in ways that no one there could have envisioned.

Embedded in the new formats and uses of history in the digital age are profound questions about historical authority itself. In these reflections, I want to consider some accommodations that historians have made to the Internet's intrusion into the understanding of history. Furthermore, I want to suggest how the new technologies, as deployed by aggressive websites and social media figures, pose real dangers to how we think—and particularly to stress their potential damage to the historical professions and to the public's comprehension of history and its significance in pursuing the common good. I don't consider myself a Luddite about these matters. My own work has benefitted enormously from the ever-increasing store of historical information, primary sources, and research aids available on the Internet, and I am grateful for it. But the historical Luddites were right to question the consequences—intended and unintended—of a new technology. So should we, especially when so much turns on the answers.

TWO

To say that there is a crisis of historical authority in the United States today is to utter a truism. Every historical claim seems to be contested on the Internet, and public understanding of academic historical interpretations is deliberately manipulated for religious, political, or economic advantage. There are several ways to approach this fundamental new antagonism that is staring our field in the face. One of them is complaisance. We have all experienced the rapid transformation of communication and information access through computers and social media. It seems simply to be a *fait accompli* that the screens have triumphed, and that might even be a good thing. There are enough websites providing critical and reliable information out there to sustain and even advance the authority of critical historical interpretation. Indeed, academic historians have come to rely on those resources to be more productive and increase the accuracy of their work. Why worry, then, that the Internet might be undermining the cultural authority of historical research?

A second response is denial. Not only historians, but also many humanists in other disciplines whom I have encountered do not believe that fundamental humanistic values are at risk today, despite the unprecedentedly rapid technological, economic, and political transformations that are under way in the United States, of which the Internet is a principal agent. This confidence, like technological enthusiasm, is not easily dismissed. It is based, after all, in the confidence scholars have in the critical interpretation of evidence that has guided the liberal arts since the Renaissance. Surely the inherent value of the ideas and institutions that critical scholarship has produced over the last seven centuries cannot be abandoned, and greater democratization of access to historical research can only advance public confidence in what is to be learned from historical study. The truth is great and will prevail, and critical doubt is the best way to seek that truth. Historical inquiry supplies endless confirmation that things do not happen simply, that human actors are complex, that contexts matter. Such knowledge frees us from the potential tyrannies of historical assumption. As the custodians of this great Western intellectual heritage, historians are responsible for the specific task of continuing to pass that knowledge and its methods on to our audiences with the greatest rigor possible. The future will be safe in their hands.

THREE

Complaisance and denial will not suffice. The inaccurate and biased historical claims that Stout warned about have found a potent and aggressive new vehicle in digital communication, including the Internet broadly and social media specifically, which can promote powerful new public narratives of the past that threaten to overwhelm both the critical accounts that historians produce and the cultural institutions that give them professional sustenance. How has this happened? My own view is that the collapse of historical authority is part of a much larger disintegration of the framework of ideas, values, and institutions that have guided American culture for a century. Several factors have combined to produce this breakdown and facilitate its replacement by a far more anarchic, arbitrary, and unstable relationship among knowledge, scholarship, and public discourse that is dissolving the very possibility of a shared historical narrative for the nation. None of these factors has been more powerful than the rise of the Internet and digital communication technologies.

There is a necessary epistemological determinism in digital technology that shows itself in both its design and use-value. Screen-and-page formats tend to equalize content and thereby legitimize it for unaware users. Search engines are, in fact, preference and marketing tools, so that what you get in response to your search is filtered and calibrated to your supposed interests, based on your previous search profile, not exclusively on the question you asked. Texting has fostered a new argot of abbreviated, contracted communication, and Facebook has linked open-ended legions of "friends" together for good or ill. And, of course, there is the tyranny of 140 characters, arbitrarily imposed on the planet by Twitter. What exactly can you say that is at all meaningful in 140 characters, given that this sentence alone takes up 122 of them? In the ten short years of Twitter's existence, brief, over-generalized, and fallacious claims about the past have scrambled the public's understanding of historical meaning, substantially subverted professional journalism, and become the blunt instrument of Donald Trump's presidential campaign and early administration.

The rise of digital communications has simplified and coarsened our language, shortened our attention spans, and filtered our access to information. These engineered limitations have epistemological consequences. They diminish the human intellect and militate against our confrontation with human complexity and the critical interpretation of history. There are, of course, exceptions to these trends in online historical publications, from blogs to essays to new journals. But the larger tendency of the technology and its relentlessly utilitarian applications is to produce what Evgeny Morozov has called the "Net Delusion."[1] On the one hand, digital technology and social media leave many users feeling less significant, less informed, and less able to affect the future. On the other hand, the deterministic channeling of information has encouraged extreme religious, political, and cultural interpreters on the Internet to manipulate the thoughts and feelings of the alienated.

At least as hazardous to the idea of historical authority are the utopian schemes of universal knowledge being actively pursued in America's tech sector. The best known is artificial intelligence (AI). IBM's Watson and other prototypes contain an ever-increasing proportion of the world's knowledge and are acquiring the capability for human linguistic expression and human-like judgments of fact and value. This technology was not developed so that you can turn on your television with a word of command to an ostensibly friendly little device. What now appears to be convenient automation through "the Internet of things" can readily become a slippery slope to the gradual replacement of human reckoning by machines. And if you want to learn how connected you already are to the supercomputers of Google, Yahoo, or the National Security Agency and how impossible it is to get unplugged, read Julia Angwin's harrowing account in *Dragnet Nation: A Quest for Privacy, Security, and Freedom in a World of Relentless Surveillance*.[2]

Still more alarming is the Singularity, a favorite concept among Silicon Valley's digital giants. This vision sees the development of AI as the springboard for a new phase of sociobiological evolution in which super-intelligent machines will supersede the possibilities of human evolution by having the ability to replicate and control their own development entirely free of human intervention. In this scenario, history will simply be irrelevant—except, perhaps, for the history of the Singularity itself, which will be written, of course, by the machines. In one variation of the Singularity, described by Jaron Lanier in *You Are Not a Gadget: A Manifesto*, devices implanted in human brains will all be connected to super-intelligent machines to produce a common consciousness, in which each one of us will know everything and be able to create action in the world simply by thinking it.[3] What would history mean in such a world, and what sort of authority could it possibly have for the humans whose story it proposed to narrate and construe?

FOUR

The Internet was originally sold to the American public as a utopian venture that would both democratize and elevate our culture by providing instant, comprehensive, and accurate information. By the time I attended the Yale conference in 1991, our speaker was giving the lie to that pious hope. What has happened since has indeed been democratization, but to paraphrase Jimmy Carter, we have gotten an Internet that is as good, or as bad, as our people. The networking capabilities of Facebook and Twitter, along with a near-universal opportunity to create personal websites, have allowed every citizen everywhere to communicate with the entire world. Among the most prominent consequences of this capability are the rise of the Darknet, which facilitates criminal activity of all sorts, and the proliferation of trolls whose specialties are lying and bullying. The utopian Internet has turned dystopian, becoming an unprecedented medium of communication whose lack of constraints has created moral and intellectual anarchy.

More significant than even this alarming development is the transformation that universal communication has wrought on the cultural status of knowledge itself. For millennia, knowledge has been nurtured by intellectual methods, preserved by specialists, and passed on from generation to generation. The epistemological corollary of such knowledge is continuity: what is known must be consciously passed on within a mutually shared framework of comprehension. The custodians of such knowledge exercised cultural authority because they knew important things that most people did not, and they understood what they knew as part of a historical process of inquiry and reflection. In just the past few decades, however, knowledge has been transmuted, as if by alchemy, into information.

The master alchemist has been the Internet, but the transformation it has wrought has turned gold into lead. Information requires interpretation, but in the digital age every Internet user is a sovereign interpreter, a situation that leads to cognitive anomie. Cognitive anomie is not the same as the more familiar concept of historical relativism. The latter acknowledges legitimate differences between interpretations of the same historical event, person, or movement, but the legitimacy of those differences depends upon a larger shared context of interpretive self-awareness, a methodological framework that demands critical discourse about how and why a historical interpretation is being made. Cognitive anomie, by contrast, is historical assertion precisely without this common framework of disciplined understanding. It claims historical truth without acknowledging or even being aware of the need for explanation; it presents historical truth as if it were just information, which can be true or false. This lack of a methodology that rationalizes interpretation unhinges historical authority from historians and vests it in the arbitrary presentation of "facts" as if they had self-evident meaning. This cognitive anomie in turn creates opportunities for powerful Internet-assisted forms of cultural fundamentalism to be deployed by anyone who wants to promote them for any reason.

FIVE

One of the most striking disclosures at the Massachusetts Historical Society's recent workshop on the future of history was the sharply different readings of historical prospects today by academic historians and administrators of public history sites and programs. Senior academic historians reported dwindling enrollments in the undergraduate major and a decline in the number and quality of applicants to their doctoral programs. On the other hand, curators of public historical sites and directors of state historical societies said that the number of visitors and participants in their programs has been solid and is increasing. Popular interest in things historical is still out there and appears to be making a comeback.

These accounts point to a sharp distinction between historical authority defined publicly and historians' authority as based in the academy. This distinction has always existed in some form, and the constituency for popular history in the twentieth century, always larger than for academic history, remained consistently patriotic—military history above all, along with biography, big-picture narratives, and sites like battlefields, national shrines, and historic homes. The contemporaneous development of history graduate programs, however, secured the place of academic historians in the roster of public intellectuals and cultural commentators. With that status came the advocacy of Progressive cultural and political research agendas. Many would identify Charles A. Beard's *An Economic Interpretation of the Constitution of the United States* (1913) as marking the decisive break from filiopietistic American historical narrative and the advent of critical Progressive historiography. During the Great Depression and World War II, a succession of Progressive historians published carefully researched, elegantly written, and morally compelling studies of crucial American ideas and institutions. Their great themes were the dangers of economic self-interest and anti-intellectualism and the centrality of democratic reform in the American story. After the war, a younger generation argued that the larger vocation of the American historian was to promote what Richard Hofstadter called a liberal "consensus" about the meaning of our national experiment as an indispensable foundation for a democratic national culture.[4]

The Boomer generation, to which I belong, rebelled in the 1960s and 1970s against the hegemony of Consensus history as too limited in its research focus and insufficiently radical in its politics. We eventually gained dominance among scholars and installed our own political program of race, class, and gender as canonical subjects for historical research and interpretive redress. These academic research agendas, like those of the Progressives before them, reflected political and moral imperatives: race and civil rights, class and economic justice, gender and feminism—and, later, LGBT rights. While these agendas developed into full-fledged research specialties and subfields, public historians faced the more difficult task of curating the nation's historical awareness by blending the new interpretive emphases together with traditional narratives. Their sustained achievement over the past several decades, using a modulated approach that raised critical issues without abandoning the constructive and inspirational dimensions of the American story, has arguably made the greatest contribution to maintaining the role of historical authority as a foundational element in our civil society.

For most of the American Century, historians played a key role in aligning the university and humanistic scholarship with a liberal political agenda. As long as the quest for historical mandates prevailed in the academy, in government, and in public culture, historians could help maintain and shape these liberal ideals of American democracy. But America is not a land of consensus, and resistance to academic historiography persevered through the Progressive Era, the New Deal, and the Great Society to emerge in decisive new form around 1980. The complaint of these resisters was that politicized academic historians excluded, even rejected, crucial traditional American values in their interpretations of the nation's past. This historiographical reaction helped facilitate the confluence of two great cultural reactions: the bicentennial revival of Evangelical religion from 1974 to 2000 and the election of Ronald Reagan in 1980. Both movements were organized around an alternative narrative of American history as the record of a divinely guided nation. One of the most influential iterations of this providentialist narrative has been the trilogy *God's Plan for America* (1977–1998) by Peter Marshall, Jr., and David Manuel, which has sold millions of copies and is still vigorously marketed and widely consumed.[5]

The argument of such books is not new. *God's Plan for America* stands in direct succession to John Winthrop's "A Modell of Christian Charitie" (1630) and Cotton Mather's *Magnalia Christi Americana* (1702), offering a dramatic account of American ascension and declension as the chosen people of the deity. The trope, of course, is biblical—a fusion of the history of ancient Israel with the jeremiads of the prophets. When the people live in faith to the divine will, the nation prospers; when they disobey, the nation falls into degeneracy and decline. Only a revival of the people's faith can restore it to God's favor. This covenantal myth has been a permanent part of America's civil religion since Mather's time, and its appeal continues today, especially because it can accommodate times of both national success and failure.

By the turn of the twenty-first century, the providentialist myth was locked in a struggle for cultural hegemony with academic history. The advent of the Internet has given a huge advantage to the former, because myth is far more easily converted into short, simplified messaging and factional sloganeering than is critical narrative. The tendency of the net to create "silos" or "echo chambers," in which cultural groups talk only to themselves and thereby legitimize their assumptions, has also dramatically amplified the intensity and integration of theo-historical traditionalists, while "elite" readers of academic history remain individuated by their critical training to be suspicious of every interpretation.

In Donald Trump's presidential campaign, a decisive change occurred in this historiographical alignment. The alt-right, with its quasi-

Christian rhetoric laced with white supremacist beliefs, linked up to the larger Christian nationalist constituency through Trump's candidacy. As the career of Trump consigliere Steve Bannon amply illustrates, alt-right commentators have no interest in historical method or even facticity. They will, and indeed did, invent facts about any issue, including wholesale denials of historical reality, while viciously attacking anyone who stands up for an interpretation of our past that does not justify their political assumptions. This alt-right mythography readily blended with the Christian nationalist narrative. Trump's campaign slogan, "Make America Great Again," perfectly captured the essence of this new version of providentialist myth: we have declined from the national glories of the 1950s, the moment has come to reverse our declension, we will take our country back from the undemocratic educated elite and alien minorities of every kind, we will restore the Golden Age, and blessings will surely follow.

Some months ago, the purveyors of this nationalist myth won the 2016 election, with the crucial aid of hostile, expedient, and amoral Internet trolls from the alt-right who enjoy disrupting cultural order and intellectual discourse, either for the hell of it or for the sake of promoting an Americanized form of neo-Nazi propaganda. With political legitimacy, they will now try to extend their appropriation of historical authority and their attack on academic historians. Hofstadter's consensus is more than broken. It is shattered into mere shards floating in the Internet culture, with profound potential harm to American democracy.

SIX

One of the most critical and contentious issues about the design of the American republic is whether the Founders presupposed a shared moral and intellectual norm of civic virtue among the people as a necessary condition for the proper functioning of republican government. The writings of George Washington, John Adams, Thomas Jefferson, and James Madison endorsed this concept of republican virtue and called for its inculcation chiefly through common education in history. Jefferson gave this view classic expression, writing in his Bill for the More General Diffusion of Knowledge (1779) that "the most effectual means of preventing [the perversion of power into tyranny] would be to illuminate, as far as practicable, the minds of the people at large, and more especially to give them knowledge of those facts, which history exhibiteth, that possessed thereby of the experience of other ages and countries, they may be enabled to know ambition under all its shapes, and prompt to exert their natural powers to defeat its purposes."[6]

In the second half of the twentieth century, however, a different concept became dominant, in which whatever values the people hold individually or collectively are ipso facto legitimate. Today's liberals endorse this view because they believe that diversity constitutes greater democratic representation in the public sphere. Conservatives share it because they believe they are the nation's majority and that in this formula the majority view will dominate. Both sides reject the need for a constituting, historically defined moral and cultural framework for republican government that challenges all factional imperatives. Indeed, they attack such claims as intrinsically anti-democratic.

Our recent national elections have fashioned sovereign individualism and factional interests into adversarial formulations of public values with ever-greater political polarization and ever more urgent efforts to undo the previous administration's ideals and actions. The presidential sequence of Kennedy/Johnson, Nixon/Ford, Carter, Reagan, Clinton, Bush, Obama, and Trump expresses not the continuity of a framing national moral identity but rather a conflict between two increasingly differentiated and self-contained systems of meaning and purpose. The narrowness of the divide cannot be more dramatically expressed than in the closeness of our elections in 1960, 2000, and 2016. This is not the people's consensus of virtue at work but rather what Michael Kammen called the "bi-formity" of the American order in his precocious 1983 book, *People of Paradox.*[7] We now rely on the slender thread of institutional order and customary practice to get us by, instead of a common sense of the common good. As I write this, those political institutions and customs are under direct attack by the Trump administration.

With extreme individualism and categorical polarization prevailing in our national culture, cognitive anarchy attending our primary means of communication through the Internet and social media, and anti-democratic forces using this combination to undermine our political institutions and practice, the need for a genuine moral consensus and a vision of common purpose is more urgent now than perhaps it has ever been. As Jefferson and Hofstadter rightly said, historians can and must help to construct that consensus, because history matters and its careful interpretive adjudication is a necessary component of any common frame of reference for political self-government. But neither a vacuous and isolated individualism nor a pernicious myth of factional fiction will inform the citizenry adequately about America's historical meaning. Nor will a privileged liberal academic historiography.

The task of consensus building once again falls to historians, among others, but how might we accomplish it? A vigorous engagement in public history is one obvious answer. The first order of business should be to reconnect our narratives to the people's interests without forfeiting the rigor of our interpretive methods. Train graduate students so that they can administer historical and cultural sites as well as parse postmodern theory. Create websites that check and correct false historical claims by public and private figures. Encourage writing that is accessible to more than a few hundred specialist readers. Conceive studies of historical figures, communities, and movements that have been left out of the race-class-gender agenda. Interrogate, understand, and critically interpret those who have felt excluded from historical research and interpretation. Above all, speak directly to the need for a new historical consensus for twenty-first-century America and attempt to build it.

The agenda for historians today demands not only continuing the careful work that preserves our canons of methodological rigor; it also demands the far more difficult task of persuading many more citizens that "history" is neither arbitrary nor simply informational but is rather the people's discourse about their past, that historical knowledge helps to define the shared values the Republic requires, that the academic training of historians does not make them political and cultural elitists, and that Jefferson was right to insist that history's scrupulous interpretation enables the people "to know ambition under all its shapes, and prompt [them] to exert their natural powers to defeat its purposes."

The imperative of twentieth-century historiography continues with even more urgency in the twenty-first. Historians are called today to reclaim historical authority and help create a new national consensus that joins past and present, rich and poor, Left and Right, even sacred and secular, and brings together all races, genders, and communities in a vision of public virtue, national purpose, and the common good for America. As the Founders knew, only a set of principles grounded in reason, morality, and history can unite such a disparate and fractious nation. The challenge is daunting, but once again we must write history in order to make history.

1 Evgeny Morozov, *The Net Delusion: The Dark Side of Internet Freedom* (New York, 2011).

2 Julia Angwin, *Dragnet Nation: A Quest for Privacy, Security, and Freedom in a World of Relentless Surveillance* (New York, 2014). See also Maggie Jackson, *Distracted: The Erosion of Attention and the Coming Dark Age* (Amherst, N.Y., 2008).

3 Jaron Lanier, *You Are Not a Gadget: A Manifesto* (New York, 2010).

4 Richard Hofstadter, *The American Political Tradition* (1948; New York, 1989).

5 Peter Marshall, Jr., and David Manuel, *The Light and the Glory: 1492–1793* (1977; Grand Rapids, Mich., 2009); *From Sea to Shining Sea: 1787–1837* (1986; Grand Rapids, Mich., 2009); *Sounding Forth the Trumpet: 1830–1865* (New York, 1997).

6 Julian P. Boyd et al., eds., *The Papers of Thomas Jefferson* (Princeton, N.J., 1950–), 2:526–527.

7 Michael Kammen, *People of Paradox: An Inquiry into the Origins of American Civilization* (Ithaca, 1990).

Ellsworth H. Brown   Balancing Multiple Income Streams

BALANCING multiple income streams is not chiefly about the money. The well-worn phrase "Everything affects everything else," attributed variously to Buddha and other philosophers, claimed by motivational authors and speakers, and cited by physicians, may best summarize the elastic complexity of this subject. Balancing income streams is about sources of money that can complement and converge or compete, control or provide freedom, provide stability or stasis or instability, and constantly shift underfoot, depending sometimes on chance and sometimes on the ever-changing vagaries of personal and public preferences, trends, and values.

In short, balance is about meeting the wants and needs of audiences. If one accepts that in most instances financial support of museums, historical societies, colleges, and universities is discretionary in degree if not wholly so, then this position is inherently correct.

Categories of income appear straightforward, are easily catalogued, and include government operating funds, grants from private and public sources, gifts from private sources, and earned income. Capital

Ellsworth H. Brown, Ruth and Hartley Barker Director of the Wisconsin Historical Society, was formerly President of the Carnegie Public Library Pittsburgh and CEO of the four Carnegie Museums of Pittsburgh. He previously directed the Chicago Historical Society, the Tennessee State Museum, and the Dacotah Prairie Museum (Aberdeen, S.D.). Dr. Brown has served on several boards and commissions of the Smithsonian Institution and is a former president of the American Association of Museums.

funds for maintenance and repair and for new construction and expansion share similar sources, with some exceptions such as bonds, but are not considered in this discussion. However, much of what follows applies to them as well. Also not addressed are funding sources for colleges and universities, and to a certain degree academic historians, because of the scale of these institutions and the pan-institutional nature of their funding sources.

Holding a discussion of income streams up to the table of contents of this publication suggests the breadth of connections to be found in, for example, the pieces by John Lauritz Larson, Richard Rabinowitz, and Dennis Fiori. The reverberation between income streams and the fundamental missions and activities of a given agency can be intense.

This contribution will address first the several income streams and their complexity and then turn its attention to several miscellaneous but essential subjects and suggestions.

GOVERNMENT OPERATING FUNDS may come from any public source—town and city, county, state, or federal. As considered here, this source comprises general funds that cover personnel, programs, building maintenance and rent, and so forth. The funds tend to be consistent over time, although there are stark exceptions to this. By this definition, they are also unrestricted in that they are not directed to a specific project or initiative, and they are almost always provided by the source's principal tax base through annual or biennial budgets.

It is possible but highly unusual for public operating funds to be the sole source of income for an institution. And while it may be tempting to wish that this were the case, it can be a double-edged sword. Andrew Carnegie insisted on continuing public financial support for libraries, but he referred to museums as "necessary luxuries" and did not insist on their support via public money. This attitude and the associated perception that in times of financial crisis, such as after 2008, cultural institutions rate second to essential public services for health, human welfare, and human safety led to major and sometimes total defunding. Several dominant state historical societies suffered financially or were dismantled following the recession. And agencies of any size that failed to make an indelible impression of essential purpose on governing bodies—executives, legislatures, commissions, and councils—were the most likely to suffer.

The pendulum does swing, however, and one will read elsewhere in this publication that state agencies, for example, are on the rebound. In fact, new homes or support facilities for historical agencies are under construction, recently completed, or planned for Tennessee, Alaska, Colorado, New Mexico, Idaho, and Wisconsin, among other places. And herein lie several truths.

First, the shockwave that blanked the field in 2008 spurred many historical agencies into concerted efforts to reach out to their broad public audiences. This is a trend that will not soon be set aside. It contributed to the rebound, and though it is perceived largely through personal narratives within the profession, these narratives are widespread and consistent, as was evident at the symposium that is the source of this publication.

Second, the recovery demonstrates that, despite temporary setbacks, the histories of communities (whatever their size) are fixed in the lives and minds of their residents. If one scans history-based channels, films, documentaries, public programs in libraries and schools, and the steady flow of prize-winning history books on the national market, as well as any programming or communication that stresses the genetic side of genealogy, one will find abundant evidence of history's staying power in the general populous, despite declining enrollment in college and university history programs. Indeed, history is a perpetual growth business, as can be seen from family or personal perspectives, community or organizational perspectives, and the always fresh sweep of national presidential history. This redounds to the credit of historical museums and societies regardless of their size.

Third, the swing of the pendulum also suggests that the goodwill toward and trusted nature of historical agencies is largely intact. It is now well documented, for example by a 2017 summary of "Museum Facts" by the American Alliance of Museums, that of all sources of information—corporate, governmental, and institutional—museums (and history museums especially) score highest in ratings of trust. This suggests a fundamentally audience-centric reputation, which should be cultivated and protected at all costs.

There are other dimensions of public funding that also need to be addressed, however. One of the ways in which museums can maintain the public's trust or avoid the ire of funding sources is to eschew the depths and winding ways of analytic discourse and exhibitions that confront head-on subjects that are current and controversial in the public mind, those that confront hard truths. To put it differently, it is safer to trade in long-resolved and positive aspects of history, safe zones, and happy and heroic stories. Some agencies, of course, have legitimate and close links to this long view of history by virtue of their own histories, collections, and facilities.

Professionals working in an historical agency must—or perhaps should—make a conscious and strategic decision about which of two roads to traverse . . . no Frostian decision here, but rather the sharp division between a civic duty to deal in the stories that cement the elements of a civil society—cohesiveness, shared stories, a positive sense of one's place in a community—and a social or moral obligation to confront hard truths, questions of tolerance and inclusion, right versus wrong, consequences and meaning in changing social and economic frames. The debate is hard to launch, harder to control, and often challenging to achieve in organizations that could anticipate high risks in responding to contemporary questions. The tension is compounded by the absence of a single "correct" answer to the question.

Consider the risk of sole-source government funding. On the one hand, there is but one element to manage. On the other, there may be stability in spreading the risk among a variety of sources: when one indicator falls, another may step in. But there is another risk too, presented here as an apolitical analysis. According to a 2017 report by Rutgers University's Center on the American Governor, Republicans control thirty-one of the states' legislatures and thirty-three governorships. Republicans control the legislatures and governorships combined in twenty-four states.

Without judging whether a governing philosophy is right or wrong, it is nonetheless evident that the dominant agenda in America is now reduced spending, smaller and more efficient government, and taxes in stasis or reduction. The question is not only whether a museum or historical society wants to accommodate this picture—keeping in mind that governments have the power and the right to require or enforce adjustments by a wide variety of means. No, the more functional question is whether it *can* do so in a timely fashion. The only truly nimble area of change is collecting, which can quickly accommodate changing values and ensure even-handed collections that will reinforce an institution's reputation as a reliable source of information.

The answer to the question just posed depends on several things, and this may be the proper place to contemplate the nature of three intersecting forces. Imagine three leaves of a common plant with elliptical leaves, say goldenrod or American elm. Now imagine that the tips of these leaves, laid on a piece of paper, intersect. To the degree that they overlap, the fuller the intersections of the bodies, the stronger the complementary connection.

Now imagine that one of these leaves represents an organization's assets: building, collections, size or skill of staff, reputation in community, range of programs, budget, membership. These are the tools with which an institution works, and for the most part they are the least able to change and adapt quickly.

The second leaf represents the wants and needs of audiences. The potential range of these elements is vast. Most agencies cope well with the essential components: genealogy, lectures, exhibitions, group tours, children's programs, and so forth for core audiences. The ability (limited by assets) to go beyond tried-and-true, to move from *more* to *different* audiences, and to explore different methods of delivery (consider the climb up the digital mountain) is expressed by a rapidly rising curve of challenges.

It is the third leaf that poses the greatest challenge, because it represents an institution's values. It is the one that confronts society's changing employment patterns, legislative initiatives, economic models, technology and its STEM classmates, and demographics, and it also accommodates millennials' expectations and new ways of communicating.

The third leaf comprises historical values shared by academe and historical agencies; institutional values attendant to agencies' embrace of audiences and related programs; and the values endemic to their own performance, governance, and management history. Given two leaves that resist rapid change and adaptation, the last leaf of values makes developing a strategic accommodation of change possible. As the leaves slide over each other to find the ideal match of overlap and intersection, the values leaf can move the farthest. It is purely conceptual, not subject to concrete answer or clear parsing; it is open to the influence of emotions, feelings, resistance, or discovery—all hard things to submit successfully to a strategic planning task force, hard things that as often as not are resolved by informed convictions. It is the value leaf that depends on properly determining the difference between what audiences want and what they need.

Or perhaps it would have been easier to just tell a simple story, in which the Chicago Park District–based museums' directors, as a team, began the presentation to the Chicago Park District Commission of a rehearsed case for increasing funding for their museums about twenty-five years ago. In that quintessential political city, from the quintessential commission, came the lasting explanation of government relations: "We think all of you are a fine asset to the city, and if you need more money, all you have to do is convince our constituents and you've got it."

WHAT ABOUT THE OTHER streams of income? Grants represent a less complex challenge, principally because they are usually project- or program-specific, often situational. Some—especially federal grants, such as those that support states' historic preservation programs—are formula-based and until now have been relatively stable over time. Others are sought and earned competitively. The latter require a sensitivity to national trends embedded, say, in the National Endowment for the Humanities, but this is learnable and usually comes with the assistance of the granting agency's staff.

Securing grants often involves an intense or focused effort. Fortunately, most efforts are time-limited and program-specific, and the pivot to new trends or initiatives can occur relatively quickly, garnering financial assistance that can enable change. This is in contrast to the effort it takes to sustain large, repeating, and sometimes threatened sole-source operating funds.

The pattern just mentioned applies not only to federal grants but also, for the most part, to foundation grants, such as those awarded by community foundations. As a general but not universal rule, however, the closer to home a source of funds is, the more likely it is to prefer programs that meet specific, local social needs. If an historical agency identifies an intersection between its mission and such needs, the results can be very good. The risk to avoid is the rationalization of a new direction without the necessary strategic decisions attendant to it—decisions that can help avoid a second risk, the use of funds of uncertain continuance to launch a new direction without a clear sense of a source for continued funding. It is unusual for most granting agencies, or for that matter corporations and individuals, to continue support for an initiative indefinitely.

Corporate income streams usually offer greater clarity. Many corporations are motivated by the desire to serve the public good, but rarely is this uncoupled from a direct benefit to the corporation as well. In fact, many corporate gifts are made via marketing budgets that directly serve corporate missions. This relationship isn't bad; it can often be good . . . and when grants are made to the larger and most prestigious organizations, one happy outcome of the mutual association is the public affiliation of the two, the reputation and mission of each complementing the other. In these relationships, it may be possible for the historical agency to share the creation or management of the program with the business. But it is also possible that the playing field is uneven and that a corporation might attempt to exercise undue influence on the historical product, to its detriment.

Fortunately, agency-to-business relationships are usually relatively transparent and thus easier to manage well. And contrary to latent beliefs, close associations can be spectacular: imagine the world-class scientific abilities of Westinghouse coupled with a neighboring science center, for example, or an international brewer's assistance in establishing an historic brewery on a rural site. Symbiotic mutual gain could be the brass ring of a relationship.

Another source, earned income, deserves a much more aggressive and sophisticated look than many agencies have been prepared to give it, although this appears to be changing rapidly and for the better. It is income derived from the sale of merchandise, services, or spaces, or perhaps income from a patent . . . almost always income from transactions.

A quick review of innovations in digital integrated business systems, the practice of using consultants, and evolving marketing techniques will reveal that virtually all historical agencies—and more so, the smaller they are—are significantly behind the for-profit world. A diversion of funds or a campaign to support dramatic modernization in an institution can often be adopted with numbers that clearly demonstrate the scale of success and the value proposition of such an effort.

The good news? The private sector stands ready to work its magic for a specific and knowable fee, with skills many agencies have yet to dream of. New systems can connect to membership databases, store inventories, attendance, reservations and ticket sales, and more. They can provide data on attendance patterns, visit time, demographics, travel patterns, and responses to advertising. The bad news? Unfortunately, the scale of an organization must be sufficient to reap the rewards of such a system, precluding practical participation by smaller operations. It may be possible to overcome this obstacle through the collaboration of several nonprofit organizations that have decided to pool their resources.

In the realm of earned income, the possibilities are many, if situational: some facilities are conducive to rental—for some reason, barns remain a popular venue . . . and once married in a museum or historic site, the couple and their guests will never forget that institution. Other facilities can corner the regional genealogy market or offer scanning lessons. Still others sell photographs or replica goods. Mitigation of risk can be achieved by gathering a deep body of transactional knowledge about audience preferences and desirable products and services, with which technology can help.

To realize the usefulness of marketing as it applies to earned income, it may be helpful to keep in mind its three elements: 1) identifying and understanding the wants and needs of the customers; 2) creating or making available the things that meet those needs, at a reasonable price point, while not sliding the third leaf improperly far; 3) telling the identified customers that the product is available. (It is often thought that number 3 constitutes "marketing," and this would be a very limiting condition.) Again . . . the market will rule.

Finally, income from membership and attendance and the charitable giving of individuals often makes up the bulk of contributed funds—significantly more than corporate giving or giving by partnerships such as law firms. In this realm more than in any other, the fundamentals are critical. The receiving institution's reputation and community standing, its historical integrity, and its financial condition and accountability are the assets most important to success.

As a rule, large, private donors give most willingly to institutions they trust and that harbor values in alignment with their own. They give because they believe in the institution's mission and its ability to do things in a community that the donors also believe in but cannot execute at scale except through giving. And members join because they support the institution's mission, perhaps even more than because they appreciate the benefits. A hint of discord or, worse yet, a scandal of any kind—about employees, financial accountability, collections anomalies—or criticism can shut down a donor's empathy quickly or, at best, lead to doubt: "We'd prefer to wait awhile before considering another contribution."

There may be no institution that will represent itself as having a sufficient endowment. But even the allure of a continuous stream of money can occasionally use tempering. One million dollars will beget an annual payout, based on a three-year rolling average of the portfolio's holdings, of a modest $40,000. If funds can be raised only incrementally over time, it may be possible to invest, say, $500,000 in a game-changing initiative or adjustment in the institution instead, thereby creating a greater earned income afterward.

The best development of all income streams discussed above is achieved through interpersonal contact on a regular basis over time. Lobbying, sales and rentals, the bonds of a guided trip taken together, and partnerships with for-profit entities can have a powerful effect. Development visits cannot be episodic, with years between connections. They must be able to demonstrate friendship, forward progress, and need surrounded by success, and they must also avoid a crisis. Achieving all of this requires skill, training, and experience. It requires consistent and timely commitment. And when done well, the management of income streams—the management of the people who superintend the streams—changes the face of an organization.

Balancing multiple income streams requires compromises informed by attentiveness to friendships and changing societal values . . . museums and historical agencies may not be at the center of governmental power (although we sometimes get lucky), but they can always be nimble, smart, and the best of partners. They can create lasting and cherished public-private partnerships for the greater good of society.

Marilynn S. Johnson

Teaching History in a Brave New World

FOR THOSE OF US concerned about the future of history, the sharply declining enrollment in college history courses has been an alarming trend. The sustained drop in the number of graduating history majors, which began with the great recession of 2008, has not yet subsided. In fact, the most recent data shows that the number of history majors dropped by 9.1 percent from 2013 to 2014 and that history course enrollments dropped by 7.9 percent between the 2012–2013 and 2014–2015 school years. Large research universities and prestigious liberal arts colleges have seen the steepest declines.[1]

But the gloomy outlooks of academic historians who attended the Massachusetts Historical Society's Future of History workshop in 2016 were offset by the more upbeat appraisals of public historians. For many of the latter, there has been no drop-off in the public's appetite for history. Their audiences are as large as ever and growing. The much-vaunted opening of the National Museum of African American History and Culture in Washington, D.C., in 2016 and the debut of the Museum of the American Revolution in Philadelphia are both testaments to the abiding public interest in history. If we consider all

Marilynn S. Johnson is Professor of History at Boston College. She is the author of several books, including *The New Bostonians: How Immigrants Have Transformed the Metro Area since the 1960s* (2015). She is also the founder of Global Boston, a new digital project on urban and immigration history.

the exciting new digital projects and platforms available on the web, the future of history appears far brighter than the academic statistics suggest.

So why the lagging interest in history courses and majors? As many have suggested, the recession and its slow recovery have been largely to blame. The prospect of finding work in a tight job market has prompted many undergraduates (often pressured by their parents) to avoid history and other humanities majors in favor of economics, business, or STEM fields. The ability to land jobs immediately after graduation has become even more important as students carry increasingly large debt loads. For many working- and middle-class graduates, the once viable path of low-paid internships supplemented by part-time service work simply does not cover the loan payments and bills in expensive metropolitan areas. I believe student interest in history is still strong, but many are now minoring in history or double majoring with what's seen as a more "practical" major, such as economics.

Meanwhile, the sustained loss of history majors even as the economy improves *is* cause for concern. Without healthy student enrollments, academic hiring gets put on hold, retired colleagues are not replaced, our new PhDs cannot find jobs, and course offerings shrink. Soon, the interest and excitement around history that students develop through their coursework may dwindle as the downward spiral continues.

Academic leaders have argued that the enrollment problem is mainly a matter of communication and marketing. American Historical Association (AHA) Executive Director James Grossman notes that, in the long term (ten to twenty years), history majors actually earn salaries comparable to those of business majors. Moreover, as we know, the critical-thinking, research, and writing skills that the study of history entails are essential qualities for success in the corporate, government, and nonprofit sectors. We need to do a better job, many argue, of selling the virtues of the history major to both students and parents, as well as combatting the shortsighted comments of politicians who denigrate the liberal arts.[2]

True enough. But as historians, we cannot deny that the larger social context is changing, and changing fast. Many of the typical careers that history majors once pursued have been contracting. De-clining resources for public education and disrupted business models in fields like law, publishing, and journalism have meant fewer jobs for history grads. At the same time, though, new opportunities are opening for those with the right skills and experience. Most obviously, the digital frontier has been expanding at a furious pace, and the potential for tapping into new sources of big data offers an array of new research possibilities. In this complex world, the critical-thinking and writing abilities of history students are certainly invaluable, but so too are other skills in a fast-changing organizational and technological landscape.

A recent study by the AHA's Career Diversity Initiative, funded by the Andrew W. Mellon Foundation, identified five traits that historians need to succeed in the non-academic job market. Although the study focused on PhDs looking for alternatives to academic employment, the findings are relevant for undergraduate history majors as well. The five traits are (1) *communication* to a variety of audiences; (2) *collaboration*, particularly with non-historians; (3) *quantitative literacy*; (4) *intellectual self-confidence* and the flexibility to use skills beyond their comfort zone; and (5) *digital literacy*, which complements all the other skills.[3] If we want to encourage more students to study history in today's world, we need to help them acquire some of these twenty-first-century skills—most of which are not commonly a part of history courses. So how can we do this?

Adding digital methods and projects to history courses is one obvious way to build digital literacy, but it can facilitate some of the other traits as well. In traditional history classes, students function mainly as individuals who listen to lectures, read and discuss materials, write papers, and take exams. These are no doubt important activities that develop writing skills and critical thinking. Collaboration, however, has increasingly become a vital aspect of many workplaces in the new economy and a hallmark of the digital age. Introducing digital group projects into coursework is one way to facilitate such collaboration.

As someone who has been experimenting with digital history in my own courses at Boston College, I have been surprised by the varying levels of confidence and aptitude that students bring to the table. Some can jump right in and quickly surpass my own (limited) abilities; others are reluctant to begin and have to be led through step by step. Although I rely on digital scholarship librarians to run initial training workshops, the tech-savvy students soon become our in-house specialists. With time set aside in class for group work and consultation, collaboration becomes a key part of the course. Even when individual students are developing separate pages or sections of a project, peer review and feedback are built into the process since much of the work is done online. Students learn from one another, and a group grade (which makes up a portion of the total project grade) encourages students to help one another produce a higher quality outcome overall.

Collaboration can also happen with those outside the classroom. A good example is a digital community history project that I recently assigned in my senior seminar in urban history. Instead of writing research papers, the students worked together on researching the history of immigration in East Boston, a neighborhood that has the highest percentage of foreign-born residents in the city and a long but poorly documented history of immigrant settlement. As outsiders to the community, however, we worked with local churches and community groups that helped introduce us to the area and some of its immigrant residents. The groups included Boston by Foot, which offered a customized walking tour of the neighborhood early in the semester, and two local Catholic parishes that connected us to immigrant residents active in their parish councils. We were also assisted by two historical organizations: the Jewish Cemetery Association of Massachusetts, which is renovating a historic cemetery chapel in East Boston for use as a community center for immigrants, and the East Boston Museum and Historical Society, which is raising funds to build a community-based history museum. Both organizations provided contacts and research leads in the neighborhood; we in turn agreed to share all our research findings and resources with them through a website the class would create.

The students, who had never done anything like this before, quickly rose to the challenge. After workshops in data retrieval and analysis, oral history, and digital methods, the students undertook investigations of particular ethnic groups—Irish, Jewish, and Italian among the older groups; and Central American, Colombian, and Southeast Asian among the newer. They combed local libraries and archives, sifted through the databases of Ancestry.com, and spent time pounding the pavement in East Boston, introducing themselves to local residents and conducting interviews in both Spanish and English. In putting together the website, they designed and co-wrote the introduction page while critiquing and editing each other's individually authored sections. The group pages incorporate little-known archival photographs, oral history interviews, and video clips of recent ethnic cultural and religious events. In the coming months, the website will become part of a larger digital immigration history project called Global Boston, which I launched in 2016.[4]

Clearly, students in the seminar gained valuable collaborative work habits and skills in communication, digital research, and curation. Much to my surprise, the students did not complain about the dreaded group project (in which the best students often resent having to pull the weight of others). Instead, the public-facing nature of the project inspired them to put their best feet forward. This was not just a term paper that would be read by me—it was part of a community partnership that would reflect on our class and on Boston College. Moreover, in creating a publicly accessible website on East Boston history, students knew that hundreds or thousands of viewers might see their work in the future. As such, they had to think about how best to communicate their ideas to a public audience, work collaboratively, and share ideas. When one student discovered a useful source or feature, they shared it with the others, who quickly looked for similar items for their own sections. This was not "copying," but rather a way of building a more unified and cohesive project. Likewise, the digitally savvy students pitched in to help others in editing and uploading oral history clips and designing their webpages. Those with the strongest writing skills took on a greater role in editing the written content. Rather than competing with one another, the students created a synergy that led to a product of which they and I could be proud.

Along the way, students also gained some experience with quantitative analysis. Those researching new immigrant groups learned how to collect and assess neighborhood-based census data from 1980 to 2015. Those writing on older European groups discovered a wealth of big data on Ancestry.com, learning how to use keyword searches to develop sample data sets on immigrants' regions of origin, residence patterns, household compositions, occupations, and workplaces. Together, we created Google spreadsheets that allowed us to document various demographic and social trends in East Boston over time. More importantly, we also learned some of the limitations of those data sources and how to work around the deficiencies and biases.

The downside, of course, is that such projects require extensive preparation and groundwork. I've had to spend considerable time learning how to use content management systems and other digital tools, in addition to many hours developing contacts and partnerships in the community. I was very fortunate to have good technical support at BC, and as a senior faculty member, I had the freedom to devote the time necessary to make it happen. For untenured faculty or those at schools with fewer resources, launching such projects would be much more difficult.

Even so, there are always ways to introduce twenty-first-century skills into the history classroom. Indeed, my own introduction to digital work began with a small-scale Wikipedia assignment several years ago. In lieu of a paper in my Western history course, I developed a list of "stubs"—short, undeveloped entries on Wikipedia—that students could choose to expand. They loved the idea that we were embracing (rather than disparaging) this popular online encyclopedia and that we could play a small role in improving it. A few years ago, Wikipedia began an education program that provided tutorials and sample assignments, while pairing college instructors with local Wikipedia Ambassadors. The latter offered free class workshops in Wikipedia protocols and editing, as well as continuous online support for the students.[5]

I learned along with them and saw some exciting results. Students engaged with the collaborative Wikipedia editing process, and many were quite proud of their finished articles. Wikipedia officially recognized several students' articles for their superior quality (earning them thousand of viewers), and one was even featured in the Wiki Edu Blog, which was later picked up by the *Washington Post*.[6] Others continued to monitor their articles after the class ended to see how much traffic they received. Just this year, I received an email from a student, now a middle school history teacher, who wrote to tell me that the article he wrote three years ago on Fort Kiowa in South Dakota had recently gotten tens of thousands of hits following the release of the movie *The Revenant* (Fort Kiowa was the jumping-off point for Hugh Glass's ill-fated journey). Clearly, students who did this assignment learned to communicate effectively with a broad public audience, learned digital skills and collaborative methods, and gained confidence in working outside their comfort zones. Tellingly, several of the students included links to their articles on their résumés and graduate school applications.

Wikipedia is just one of a growing number of crowdsourced web projects that are relatively easy to join and learn. Resources like Clio (an app that guides the public to cultural and historical sites), Citizen Archivist (a site that allows viewers to transcribe documents at the National Archives), and Freedom on the Move (a Cornell University database on fugitives from slavery using runaway ads) are just a few of a growing crop of digital projects that encourage student input. Or if you'd like to create your own crowdsourced project, Zooniverse has a project builder that helps you set it up with a step-by-step tutorial.[7]

For some, though, the barriers to digital work are too daunting. In this case, there are still ways of incorporating new skills into the history curriculum via public history projects. A few years ago at Boston College, we launched a course for history majors called Making History Public, a collaboration between the History Department and Boston College Libraries. The course combines a traditional scholarly approach to a historical topic through readings and discussion with a collaborative public history project in the form of a campus exhibition. Drawing on the special collections of BC's Burns Library as well as other local libraries and archives, students write (somewhat shorter) conventional research papers on different aspects of the designated topic. But they must also translate their knowledge into a more compact and compelling public presentation. To do so, each student pre-pares a panel of images and text on their own research, while the class works together to frame and integrate the overall presentation. The exhibitions are then mounted on the walls of the History Department the following semester.

Since 2012, we have had a dazzling array of exhibitions on subjects such as bookmaking in the early modern world, Cold War history through comic books, the evolution of Boston Common, European mapmaking from 1600 to 1860, historical monuments, World War I propaganda, and the history of Boston College. One exhibition, *Righting Historical Wrongs at the Turn of the Millennium*, examines public efforts to confront historical injustices, from efforts to redress genocide of indigenous peoples to movements against sexual slavery to truth and reconciliation commissions around the globe. Most recently, students in Prof. Robin Fleming's seminar have been collaborating with the Boston city archaeologist to create an exhibition on urban history through material culture in a course called History Down the Toi-let (as old latrines are the main sites of digs). In all of these courses, students gain valuable skills in public communication, curation, and collaboration, and some have gone on to preserve their exhibitions permanently by developing digital versions as well. Similar external partnerships around public displays of historic material have been pio-neered at Boston University, where history faculty have their classes work on curatorial projects with the Massachusetts Historical Society.

While institutional funding and support certainly make all of these projects easier, there are ways to incorporate new skills with minimal expense and support. Figuring out how to do this in a given institu-tional setting is critical. Some schools have lots of resources, others very few. But creating collaborations beyond the history department, or even beyond the university, can be one way to get that support. Wikipedia and other crowdsourcing projects offer one model, but you may also find partners in local libraries, museums, historical sites, or other nonprofits. Finally, don't forget about the existing resources of your own institution. Leveraging the expertise of librarians and ar-chivists, developing partnerships with computer science or IT departments, and brainstorming with others on campus can help create that synergy. No doubt, if we want to teach our students these twenty-first-century skills, we historians need to embrace them ourselves.

Getting historians to incorporate skill-building into our courses and majors will better prepare our students for the job market, graduate and professional school, and other endeavors. But more importantly, it will help the field of history keep pace with the increasing complexity of life and work in the information age. Our students will have the benefit of the critical-thinking and writing skills that are so desperately needed today *and* the ability to access new forms of data and communication techniques that will support and promote the fruits of their learning.

1 Julia Brookins, "New Data Show Large Drop in History Bachelor's Degrees," *Perspectives on History: The Newsmagazine of the American Historical Association*, March 2016; Julia Brookins, "Survey Finds Fewer Students Enrolling in College History Courses," *Perspectives on History*, Sept. 2016. *Perspectives* is available online via the website of the American Historical Association, www. historians.org.

2 James Grossman, "History Isn't a Useless Major: It Teaches Critical Thinking, Something America Needs Plenty More Of," *Los Angeles Times*, May 30, 2016.

3 Lincoln Bramwell, "How Historians Are Like Swiss Army Knives," *Perspectives on History*, May 2016; "The Career Diversity Five Skills," Career Diversity Resources, American Historical Association, www.historians.org.

4 See Places—East Boston on the Global Boston website at https://globalboston .bc.edu.

5 See the Resources page of the Wikipedia Education Program on the Wikimedia Outreach site: outreach.wikimedia.org/wiki/Education/Resources.

6 Caitlin Dewey, "The Most Fascinating Wikipedia Articles You Haven't Read," *Washington Post*, Nov. 5, 2015.

7 Each of these resources can be accessed online at the following URLs: Clio, www .theclio.com; Citizen Archivist (at the National Archives), www.archives.gov/citizen -archivist; Freedom on the Move, freedomonthemove.org; Zooniverse, www .zooniverse.org.

Cinnamon Catlin-Legutko

History That Promotes Understanding in a Diverse Society

"In the past, Indians have had good reason to distrust and even to scorn the professional researcher. Too often have they misinterpreted the Indian history, misrepresented their way of life. It becomes necessary now to correct the record, to write the history as it should be written, to interpret correctly the aboriginal past."

—Rupert Costo, Cahuilla (1964)[1]

FOR AS LONG as I can remember, I've been in love with museums, all kinds of museums. I was a kid raised on public television, and on vacation our family traveled to museums and historic places. Each summer in Colorado we'd visit old mining towns and trace disappearing rail lines, imagining the past and wondering what life was like way back when. We would spend vacation time researching these towns in public libraries and archives, looking for photographs that

Working in museums for more than twenty years, Cinnamon Catlin-Legutko has been a museum director since 2001. Prior to joining the Abbe Museum as President and CEO in 2009, Ms. Catlin-Legutko was the Director of the General Lew Wallace Study & Museum, where she led the organization to the National Medal for Museum Service in 2008. She served as Treasurer for the American Association of State and Local History and was the Founding Chair of its Small Museums Committee. She is currently a board member of the Maine Humanities Council and the American Alliance of Museums. At the Abbe, Ms. Catlin-Legutko co-leads its decolonization initiative and develops policies and protocols to ensure collaboration and cooperation with Wabanaki people.

showed them bustling with people. This was history that intrigued us, held our attention, and bound us together in family learning and adventure.

As I headed into my college years, I knew I wanted to work with precious collections, reveal the exciting stories that can be found in history, and inspire audiences to consider the human condition. As a museum leader, I've worked in a general history museum, a literary and Civil War historic site, and I am currently working in a Native history museum. My career was launched from an educational platform made up of training and study in cultural anthropology, archaeology, art history, and history.

I believe in museum spaces and their power to change lives, inspire movements, and challenge authority. And I have examples. The STEMinista Project at the Michigan Science Center can inspire a girl to become a scientist and cure diseases of the future. The Lower East Side Tenement Museum can influence the national conversation around immigration through its dialogue-driven visitor experiences. A traveling exhibition called *Race: Are We So Different?* can change how museums and informal learning programs approach difficult conversations about race and society. This is a power that museums hold and can wield. However, I believe museum history and modern practice are terribly problematic for communities of color and, specific to my work and the examples presented below, harmful to Indigenous communities and their ancestors. Change is long overdue.

MUSEUMS ARE COLONIZERS

"But one of the most important goals [of decolonizing museums], I believe, is to assist communities in their efforts to address the legacies of historical unresolved grief by speaking the hard truths of colonialism and thereby creating spaces for healing and understanding."

—Amy Lonetree (2012)[2]

In the historic pattern of museum work, we find non-Indigenous people acquiring the belongings and the remains of people from other cultures. Museums are colonizing spaces. As Ho-Chunk scholar Amy

Lonetree writes, "Museums can be very painful sites for Native peoples, as they are intimately tied to the colonization process."[3]

Historically, museums were built as temples of culture and art, reflecting images of Europe as the ideal. For many Euro-Americans, inclusion in a museum exhibition may instill pride and signify achievement. For colonized populations, it feels like being captured and isolated in a glass case or like being collected for display on a velvet-covered card. Natural history museums in particular used, and continue to use, classification systems to organize their contents: the "Hall of African Peoples," the "Hall of North American Indians"... you get the picture. Classifications may be convenient, but they lead to a troubling practice of "othering" by those who work in museums, people who are predominantly white, like me.

Let's unpack this term—*colonization*—for a minute. Colonization occurs when a population of invaders plants colonies in the homelands of other peoples. American colonialism is motivated by religious, political, and economic factors. People whose lands are colonized are in danger. The process leads to war, massacres, enslavement, and other atrocities. The real work of colonialism is the extraction of resources of colonized peoples. Cultures and human lives are always harmed and often destroyed during colonization. Always.

Right now, today, the United States remains in a colonial relationship with tribal communities. The invaders, the colonizers, are still here. This is a fact often overlooked by history practitioners and academics alike. As Susan Miller writes, "American historians have been loath to concede the point that the United States stands in a colonial relationship to the North American tribes whose homeland it claims." This is a key difference from Indigenous historians who have "no such aversion" to using "colonialism and colonization to explain relations between Indigenous peoples and nation-states."[4] To be clear, museums hold the spoils of colonialism: the artifacts and human remains of Native people.

The fields of history and anthropology have long crafted the narrative and the interpretation that describe Indigenous museum collections—fields dominated by Eurocentric, white voices and points of view. The history of museum representation of Native peoples begins with the development of anthropology as an academic field; modern representation stems from the late nineteenth and early twentieth centuries. Academics, especially anthropologists, earned accolades by systematically collecting American Indian material culture, that is, obtaining the authentic for museum collections.[5]

They were also removing the physical remains of Native people from execution burials, traditional burial grounds, and battlefields, and depositing the ancestors in museums. To this day U.S. collections hold the remains of an estimated half million Native American individuals, and European museums hold an equal number.[6] And while there is legislation in the United States to return the ancestors through the Native American Graves Protection and Repatriation Act, there is no such legislation (or the equivalent) requiring European repatriation.

So our perceptions of Native people and Indigenous cultures are shaped by the work of colonizers: people, like me, who are trained historians, anthropologists, and museums workers. What do the results look like in our memories and in our experiences today?

Whether as a young student or as an adult, we formulate a view of static, unchanging Indigenous cultures when we read the work of biased academic textbook writers and interact with museum exhibitions informed by the same biased voices. Certainly dioramas promote this view by depicting Indians as frozen in time and by displaying them in the same galleries as dinosaurs and other extinct animals.

Our memories may also recall Native objects defined and explained by Western scientific nomenclature and not by Indigenous categories of culture, worldview, and meaning. Exhibitions often remove the human story from the material culture on display by presenting artifacts as cold and lifeless when their meaning and purpose are intimately tied to human stories. Lastly, scholars and museum workers have homogenized Native communities into one pan-Indian group, disregarding the complexity and difference that well over five hundred Indigenous nations represent.[7]

These practices, which may have informed your memories, also dehumanize Native history and create colonizing museum spaces. In such places, emotional, spiritual, and physical harm is done when these colonized spaces and practices are not acknowledged and addressed. So it makes sense that many Native people would find American museums to be painful institutions.

DECOLONIZING PRACTICE AT THE ABBE MUSEUM

"Indigenous peoples have the right to practice and revitalize their cultural traditions and customs. This includes the right to maintain, protect and develop the past, present and future manifestations of their cultures, such as archaeological and historical sites, artefacts, designs, ceremonies, technologies and visual and performing arts and literature."

—Article 11 of the United Nations Declaration on the Rights of Indigenous Peoples (2007)[8]

What is to be done? We need to decolonize museum spaces. Undoing the harm colonization has caused is the focus of our work at the Abbe Museum in Bar Harbor, Maine.

Founded in 1928, the museum's mission is to inspire new learning about the Wabanaki Nations with every visit. A historic confederacy of tribes, the Wabanaki are the Micmac, Maliseet, Abenaki, Passamaquoddy, and Penobscot. At the Abbe, their stories are shared through changing exhibitions, special events, teacher workshops, archaeology field schools, and craft workshops for children and adults. Native community members are actively engaged in all aspects of the museum, including policymaking as members of our board. The museum greets thirty thousand visitors each year with seven year-round staff members and about a dozen seasonal staff. In recent years, with broad community support, we have grown from a small trailside museum, privately operated within Acadia National Park, to include an exciting contemporary museum, opened in 2001 in the heart of downtown Bar Harbor.

Our organizational and strategic plans ask the overarching question, what can and should our museum do that is a service to Wabanaki people? Decolonization means, at a minimum, sharing governance structures and authority for the documentation and interpretation of

Native culture. Borrowing again from Amy Lonetree, decolonizing practices at the Abbe are collaborative with tribal communities. This means that when an idea for a project or initiative is first conceived, we have a conversation with Native advisors and make sure it's a story or an activity that we have the right to share or pursue. We ask permission; we don't get halfway down the planning timeline and then check with Native advisors to learn how we're doing and if we're getting it right. And, when ideas for an exhibition or program come to us from the tribal communities, we prioritize the ideas and work collaboratively to bring them to fruition. Native collaboration needs to occur at the beginning and be threaded throughout the life of the project.

A second characteristic of decolonizing museum practices is to privilege Native perspective and voice. The vast writings on the human experience are with little exception written by white academics and observers. When we begin to prioritize and privilege the writings and observations of Indigenous scholars and informants, the story broadens, expands, shifts, and introduces a clearer and non-oppressed perspective of Native history and culture. There is room to consider academic writing and research in this practice, but when there is conflict, both points of view may be presented, so long as the non-Indigenous research is not exposing sensitive information or causing harm to communities of people and their ancestors. And to this point, I have many Indigenous academic and advisor voices to credit: Amy Lonetree, Susan Miller, Taté Walker, Jamie Bissonette Lewey, Geo Neptune, Bonnie Newsom, and Darren Ranco. Their words shaped this article and influence my thinking on a regular basis.

Lastly, decolonizing museum practices include taking the full measure of history, which ensures truth-telling. Histories of Wabanaki people connect to today's challenges. Issues of water quality, hunting and fishing rights, and mascots are connected to the past and the present. When we present this full history we have a better opportunity to identify harmful statements and practices.

There are certainly museums across the United States and even around the globe that are incorporating decolonizing practices into their operations, but through our research we've found that their efforts are typically limited to exhibition development. We're concerned about exhibitions at the Abbe as well, but we're also looking at all of our operations—including governance structures, hiring practices, collections management, and educational programming—and creating decolonizing pathways. The Abbe Museum is committed to developing decolonizing museum practices that are informed by Wabanaki people and enforced by policies, managed by protocols, and overseen by inclusive governance structures. In addition, we will have other structures in place that will maintain the museum's commitment to decolonization regardless of the players involved—foremost among them the staff, trustees, and advisors.

DEVELOPING THE SKILLS FOR DECOLONIZING WORK

"Dialogue . . . is a way of exploring the roots of the many crises that face humanity today. . . . In our modern culture men and women are able to interact with one another in many ways: they can sing, dance, or play together with little difficulty but their ability to talk together about subjects that matter deeply to them seems invariably to lead to dispute, division, and often to violence."

—David Bohm, Donald Factor, and Peter Garett,
Dialogue: A Proposal (1991)[9]

Since 2013, the Abbe staff have been working closely with Sarah Pharaon from the International Coalition of Sites of Conscience (the Abbe is a member) to develop our skills in facilitated dialogue. We anticipated that our decolonizing commitment would require us to be able to have difficult conversations with each other, our board, and our museum audiences. In particular, our visitors would regularly throw us for a loop with questions such as "Are your Indians poor?" and "Can I touch an Indian?" While the visitors may not have intended to be hurtful when asking these questions, their impact is harmful for Native and non-Native staff members working the frontline audience interface. We wondered, how best could we transition questions such as these into new learning experiences that would broadens the visitors' understanding and minimize the potential for harm in the future?

We also observed that very often if a visitor was not alone, his or her companion would recognize that a question or action was rude or offensive or should be phrased differently, and would begin to mediate or correct the speaker. Dialogue was trying to happen on its own, and we were ill-prepared as a staff to engage.

Facilitated dialogue allows personal truths to come forward, be examined and valued, and be evaluated for harmful impact. The Coalition describes the opportunity dialogue offers:

> Dialogue gives equal value to the insights drawn from personal experience and the knowledge gained from intellectual study or external sources.
>
> Dialogue requires people to surface and examine the assumptions that inform their beliefs and actions. Dialogue invites a person to learn about him or herself while learning from others.
>
> The process of dialogue requires participants to establish, protect, and maintain a culture of mutual trust.
>
> The process of dialogue assumes that it is possible for two markedly different perspectives to coexist at the same time and therefore, rejects binary, either/or thinking.[10]

Fortunately for the staff, our board of trustees is committed to developing decolonizing practices and has evolved into a "learning board," hungry for readings and guest speakers to be part of our regular meetings.[11] The board could easily have been a limiting force as we dove into this training and its applications, but it was truly the opposite.

The team skill set is still a work in progress, affected by staff transitions and limited resources. We have piloted dialogue-based programs and are gradually embedding these skills into our work. Beginning in 2017, we will create and revise all educational programming to include dialogic elements, from opportunistic dialogues to intensive, guided dialogues. Facilitated dialogue places museum-goers at a shared table where they can see themselves as part of the story, either through personal connections or universal themes. This approach to relevance not only engenders support for history, anthropology, and museology;

more importantly, it generates empathy in visitors when it connects the story to their worldview. When relevance is evident, oppressive and colonizing frameworks can be dissolved.

An intrinsic step in adopting facilitated dialogue in museum environments is to identify non-negotiables. These specify what does not constitute acceptable conversation in your museum because it may be wholly untrue, even if it is commonly espoused by visitors, or because the topic is incredibly sensitive and harmful to some people and can act as a trigger. There is a wide host of reasons why selecting non-negotiables is important for moving forward with difficult conversations. The Coalition training also cautions that recognizing a non-negotiable is to be done in a way that doesn't shut down dialogue—a delicate balance indeed and a process that was incredibly challenging for the Abbe staff.[12] Ultimately, we adopted three operational truths, or non-negotiables:

> De-humanizing thousands of generations of ancestors and Indigenous people is unacceptable and perpetuates intergenerational trauma.

> Colonization is an ongoing, harmful process.

> Wabanaki nations are sovereign nations. That sovereignty is inherent and cannot be taken or given away.

Once we put these words on a flipchart and confirmed that this is the truth of our work and that it is non-negotiable, we all became surprisingly emotional. With these three truths in hand, we can navigate academia, practice, and visitor experiences while reducing harm to Indigenous people.

Of course, this isn't the only work we needed to do to be adept at decolonizing. At the same time as our study of facilitated dialogue, we submitted ourselves to racial bias training led by internationally known social justice activist Steve Wessler. Through his careful and experienced framework, we did self-work, looking at our biases and learning how to combat them and to interact in difficult situations when micro-aggressions, misrepresentations, stereotypes, and more are expressed in direct communication and overheard conversation in our museum space and personal life. Each year we offer this training to our seasonal staff as well as any new employees who have joined the professional staff.

Our training at the Abbe continues.[13] Most recently, trustee Jamie Bissonette Lewey, Abenaki, an accomplished healing and transformative justice facilitator, led board and staff in a facilitated discussion she created on power sharing and museums. In two parts, the exercise first asked the question, "Where do museums have power in America?" The answers were wide-ranging and startling when viewed as a whole: museums have control of information and objects; they selectively disseminate information; they hold power over stories and interpretation; they determine what is and isn't "appropriate"; and they hold power over taste and aesthetics.

We followed this discussion by asking a second question, "What does power sharing look like?" The ideas we generated were motivational and achievable: a Native person would serve on all museum committees; Wabanaki cultural protocols are on par with museum best practices; academic and Native knowledge and scholarship are no longer adversarial; and our archaeology field school would be led by an Indigenous archaeologist. This discussion and others continue and are designed to reveal the work we have before us and to prioritize our next steps in service to Native people and their history, culture, and art.

When you choose to dive into decolonizing work, you must accept that you won't always get it right—there will be many missteps. Your personal need to espouse "correctness" isn't a good motivator, either. And in the scheme of museum operations, the decolonizing work won't appear as urgent as it needs to be. While the work will never be done, at the Abbe we've made the decision no longer to be complicit. We've made the decision to avoid creating harmful museum policies and practices. We've made the decision to commit to revising or reversing past practices that perpetuate harm. We've made the decision to change.

This article was adapted from a TEDxDirigo talk given on Nov. 5, 2016, by the author (www.tedxdirigo.com/talks/we-must-decolonize-our-museums).

1 Rupert Costo, "A Statement of Policy," *Indian Historian* 1, no. 1 (1964):n.p.

2 Amy Lonetree, *Decolonizing Museums: Representing Native America in National and Tribal Museums* (Chapel Hill, 2012), 5.

3 Lonetree, *Decolonizing Museums*, 1.

4 Susan Miller, "Native America Writes Back: The Origin of the Indigenous Paradigm in Historiography," *Wicazo Sa Review* 23, no. 2 (2008):9–28.

5 Lonetree, *Decolonizing Museums*, 9–10.

6 Samuel J. Redman, *Bone Rooms: From Scientific Racism to Human Prehistory in Museums* (Cambridge, Mass., 2016), 15.

7 Lonetree, *Decolonizing Museums*, 14.

8 U.N. General Assembly, Resolution 61/295, "United Nations Declaration on the Rights of Indigenous People," Sept. 13, 2007, www.un.org/esa/socdev/unpfii/documents/DRIPS_en.pdf.

9 David Bohm, Donald Factor, and Peter Garett, *Dialogue: A Proposal* (1991), www.david-bohm.net/dialogue/dialogue_proposal.html.

10 International Coalition for the Sites of Conscience, Facilitated Dialogue Training Materials, 2013 and 2016.

11 How they became a learning board is a topic for another article. This was not an overnight transition and was not without serious bumps in the road.

12 International Coalition for the Sites of Conscience, 2013 and 2016.

13 The Abbe board and staff include regular Native representation and participation, but the percentage fluctuates from year to year. The board recently developed a protocol with the goal to reach Native/non-Native parity on the board by 2021.

Dennis A. Fiori

To Merge or Not to Merge: A Cautionary Note

OBTAINING sufficient operating support is a constant struggle for a majority of America's not-for-profit cultural institutions. Societal changes have only made this quest more challenging. "Bricks and mortar" cultural institutions do not play the social role they once did. How we interact, communicate, learn, find and consume entertainment, spend our spare time, and access the news are being transformed. New forms of cultural expression are supplanting the traditional. The visual, which requires minimal effort to understand, prevails. Individual donors are choosing different causes and making their contributions in new ways. In the process, philanthropy and institutional loyalties are being upended.

All in all, uncertainty looms as the current generation of donors departs. Early signs demonstrate that many heirs are uninterested in their parents' charities. The donors who constitute this new generation are hands-on, often making targeted gifts for particular projects or seeking increased accountability. Corporations and foundations, too, have turned away from arts and culture or are seeking new returns on their gifts. For years, corporate America has been shifting its grants toward social services, youth programs, and marketing opportunities. Foundations are more invested in solving the world's problems than in supporting the budgets of local not-for-profits. Human suffering

Dennis A. Fiori is President of the Massachusetts Historical Society. Previously, he was Director of the Maryland Historical Society and the Concord Museum.

brought on by global warming, war, and the current political climate is adding to the fundraising challenge.

While these trends have been with us for a number of years, their effects are now being felt more acutely across the spectrum of academic and cultural not-for-profit institutions. Colleges are reporting a dramatic drop in donations from alumni, as much as 30 percent over the last few years at some schools. This decline is occurring as they brace for a generational softening in enrollment. The Metropolitan Museum of Art is facing an operating budget deficit of over $30 million and delaying the construction of a new wing. Many symphony orchestras are depending on fundraising after decades of relying on subscribers to pay the bills.[1]

These trends have greatly affected history institutions. To be sure, there are success stories; those that have fared well include organizations with significant, relatively stable state funding and cultural institutions that are the major players in their immediate communities, especially in wealthy suburban areas. The trend toward including more art and fashion in exhibitions has also improved the bottom line of history organizations. Still, many find their financial situation unsettled. As well as being plagued by the challenges facing most not-for-profits, they depend on small and aging donor bases that are difficult to grow. If an institution is not gate-driven, there are slim possibilities for earned income from rentals, merchandising, or other sources. Available grants may only cover discrete projects that do not match the institution's priorities. Capital is often lacking to pursue innovation or to fund marketing. Many are burdened by expensive-to-maintain historic structures, collections in need of care and accessibility, and the growing expense of technology and public outreach.

Then there is the challenge of too many institutions chasing too few dollars. Within greater Boston, for example, there are 87 history organizations, ranging from all-volunteer operations to those with a staff of over a hundred. Many have overlapping missions, trustees, and donors. The same scenario exists in communities across the country. The American Association for State and Local History estimates there are approximately 19,500 historical organizations in the United

States. Does it make sense to support so many of them, not to mention new ones opening their doors all the time? With fragile bases of support, destined to become even thinner, history organizations need to consider new operating models. If facilities and staff could be consolidated to reduce expenses and focus the small, overlapping cache of supporters toward a single entity, wouldn't institutions be able to meet operating expenses, with funds remaining for innovation and marketing? Given these questions, merger has often seemed to be the logical answer. A merger is a bold move that comes with difficult decisions, sacrifices, and anxiety. Are the results worth the trauma?

Four mergers illustrate the advantages and pitfalls of amalgamation. In order to focus on general lessons, I have chosen not to identify the institutions involved but will instead label them simply as case studies A, B, C, and D. Mergers A and B each combined numerous smaller historical institutions into a new, overarching organization. Merger C brought together two large, history-based institutions with strong aesthetic collections; D consolidated six institutions—three of them historical—under one roof. For A and B, historic structures were key to the histories of the surrounding communities. Conversely, while historic structures house parts of mergers C and D, they are not essential to the new institutions' missions.

All four mergers came about for similar reasons. By combining, the partners wanted to strengthen financial stability, achieve economies of scale and operational efficiency, improve the quality and extent of their services, heighten their image and reputation, and increase public support. In none of the four cases did the merger lead to savings, but C and D did achieve stability sooner than A and B, which today continue to pursue an anticipated reward.

Mergers A and B were hindered by the absence of institutional capacity, the liabilities that partnering organizations brought to the mergers, and a lack of sufficient planning. In these cases, it became evident soon after the official merger that, where historic structures are central to their mission, deferred maintenance would be costly. Similarly, staffing was slim or nonexistent for the individual institutions encompassed by A and B. Rather than consolidate employees, they unexpectedly had to enlarge their numbers to provide professional services to all sites. Even with more staff, the workload was burdensome because of increased responsibilities. The additional staff and deferred maintenance meant that resources required for a number of unanticipated expenses—including unifying and improving technology, phone systems, branding and marketing, and the integration of collection catalogs—stressed their operating budgets. In an unfortunate cycle, these costs ultimately led to a reduction in staff, which further magnified the problems. While expenses mounted, fundraising was slow to grow. Overlapping donors did not give the same total amount to one combined organization that they did to two or three independent ones. Expanding the donor bases became challenging as the lack of funds meant fewer new programs or activities to stimulate interest in the new organizations. The pool of donors remained modest.

With greater resources from the outset, the partners engaged in cases C and D were more systematic in their approach to exploring the ramifications of a merger before they proceeded. Each concluded significant funds would be required to merge and foresaw many of the challenges that the two smaller mergers encountered. Anticipating the need for funds to cover merger expenses from foundations or local government made a crucial difference in their financial success. Also contributing to this success was agreement among the stakeholders for C and D, particularly regarding missions and goals (factors that posed a continuing challenge for A and B). Cases C and D also benefited from having members who served on the boards of multiple institutions involved, and who had deep roots in the community, such that these individuals either advocated for or directly provided the funding to facilitate the mergers. Case C was the combination of a history museum holding a significant art and artifact collection with a museum that had its roots in history, but also housed significant decorative arts, fine arts, maritime, and natural history collections. Museum leaders decided to focus on art, with history a distant priority. The loss of a history focus has troubled many, but the new art museum has been a great success. This accomplishment has helped bring about the resources to revive the history components. Historical manuscripts and documents are being cataloged and storage conditions improved, while historic structures are being restored.

Case D comprises six institutions that have come together in one very large historic structure. Three components are history based. A significant portion of their operating start-up and ongoing funding was the result of a tax levy voted in by the community's residents. Enactment took a great deal of local support, bonding the community to the new museum center, which has become a vibrant local resource.

The simple phrase "It takes money to make money" seems to sum up this cursory inquiry into the financial benefits of mergers. While the larger mergers, backed by committed donors and strong community support, have found financial success, the two smaller combinations are making progress over a much longer timeline. They remain confident that the other benefits of merger will in time lead the way to increased financial support. Setting aside the financial goal, the smaller institutions still believe merger was the correct step. It eliminates competition among history organizations, focuses collecting efforts, and allows for a more cohesive and comprehensive telling of the community's story. Their next step in pursuit of financial stability is to "right size." This requires additional hard decisions. They need to refine their missions and goals in order to forge united constituencies and to determine what historic structures will remain important to tell the community's story versus finding alternative uses and culling collections.

This brief look at four mergers brings to the surface key elements that will increase the chances of success. The merger should meet the needs of the community, serve the institutions' core constituencies, and implement good business practice—three aims that are mutually reinforcing. The proposed partners should have similar missions and organizational cultures and some parity in their financial profiles. Rescuing a weak partner usually drags down all the others. In order for the outcome to strengthen the financial stability of the merged organization, financial and development plans need to be in place before the union. The goal should be to assure minimum donor loss and to encourage contributors who gave to more than one of the merging organizations to make a combined gift at least equal to the separate gifts. A thorough analysis is required of the strengths, weaknesses, and costs of the step from an operational standpoint. This assessment requires hard data and must take into consideration deferred maintenance of all structures, a plan for combining collections and databases, and the staff required to operate the merged organizations. Out of the review should evolve an operating plan, the decision-making process, and a timeline. It can take at least a decade to absorb all the transitions of a merger, operate as a unified whole, and find financial benefit. These aspects need to be understood by all stakeholders.

Community engagement is important and requires a strategy and plan that are well thought out. Citizens need to value the new organization, understand that services will be improved and expanded, and be willing to provide necessary support. The community has to be engaged and become invested. The goal is for the reputation and public perception of the merged organization to be a significant improvement over the individual partners. Finally, united leadership is crucial. Partner boards have to make difficult decisions about who will be retained on the merged board. This needs to be accompanied by a clear consensus on who will serve as the CEO.

While mergers provide financial stability for those who bring funds and broad support among stakeholders to the project, smaller organizations without these resources face a tough uphill battle to find financial reward. To improve their chances they need to engage in analysis and planning, along with making difficult choices to right-size the new organization. While there may be an overabundance of infrastructure chasing too few dollars among history organizations, mergers are a challenging route to financial reward.

1 See the *New York Times,* Jan. 12, 2017, p. C5, and Nov. 16, 2016, p. C1.

Conrad Edick Wright

Afterword: Lines That Connect, Not Divide

WE INTRODUCED this volume by expressing our belief that history is the province of everyone who finds meaning in the past. Academic historians, public historians, history museum curators, archivists, K–12 teachers, historic preservationists, architectural historians, documentary editors, documentary filmmakers, genealogists, re-enactors, and the audiences that they all serve belong in our universe. In their own way, so do public officeholders who take history's lessons into account when setting policy, voters who draw on history when they cast their ballots, urban planners and real estate developers who are sensitive to the past in their work, and countless others who recognize history's influences on the trials of everyday life. Some of today's challenges, such as the current faculty job crisis in academia, are specific to a single group or occupational category, but many, even most, are not. Financial constraints affect institutions of all kinds; authors, teach-

Conrad Edick Wright, former Ford Editor and Director of Research at the Massachusetts Historical Society, became the Society's Sibley Editor in 2017. He is a graduate of Harvard College (AB) and Brown University (AM, PhD). His publications include *The Transformation of Charity in Postrevolutionary New England* (1992), *Revolutionary Generation: Harvard Men and the Consequences of Independence* (2005), and *Pedagogues and Protesters: The Harvard College Student Diary of Stephen Peabody, 1767-1768* (editor, 2017).

ers, and curators all need to cultivate an audience; the promise and problems of the Internet are everyone's concern.

The shared mission for those of us who find meaning in the past is to promote the crucial role of history, no matter what form it takes. Our starting point is the recognition that although we may find history everywhere, for too many Americans it is of at best marginal interest. If public officeholders and administrators in higher education budget for new initiatives in the sciences and technology to the exclusion of history and related fields, if K–12 educators focus on high-stakes reading and mathematics testing at the expense of classroom time devoted to history, if charitable foundations and individual philanthropists relegate history to the margins, then such decisions make everyone poorer, especially those of us who understand the importance of learning from the past.

If history follows the same path toward marginalization as the classics, once the centerpiece of American education, where students developed facility in the languages that marked them as citizens of consequence and considered problems of timeless importance, then our culture is impoverished.

If public policy makers believe that they can steer our government without a full and honest understanding based in history of who we are as a people and how we relate to the rest of the world, then our nation is in jeopardy.

With much at risk, our best hope for the future of history is to work together. Let's acknowledge the importance of history education in the elementary grades and high school as the basis for further study in the field. Let's recognize the accomplishments of archivists and documentary editors, whose vital work makes possible many museum exhibitions and documentary films as well as the specialized scholarship of many college and university faculty members. Let's esteem the advanced scholarship of the history professoriate. Let's value the achievements of historic preservationists and architectural historians, who promote an appreciation of the past through all they do to keep the texture of our physical surroundings.

Let's not belittle our natural allies by deprecating their training, the audiences they serve, or the kind of work they do. Let's not define ourselves and what we do by limiting our affiliations to the narrowest of professional communities. Although associating with practitioners who share our particular training and interests can promote professional and personal growth, we diminish ourselves and our potential for influential accomplishments if we allow hyperspecialization and siloing to define the outer reaches of our ambitions. If we adopt such counterproductive practices, we are enemies to our own welfare as well as to that of our society and our culture, which depend on our goodwill as well as our best efforts to assure that our leaders and citizens alike will be fully informed as they address the future's challenges.

For the future of history relies upon our commitment to promoting the qualities and values we share—the lines that connect us—and setting to one side those that divide us. When we make common cause on behalf of history, our nation and our culture are the winners.

Acknowledgments

THIS VOLUME HAS GROWN out of a workshop held at the Massachusetts Historical Society in the fall of 2016. Convened on September 8–9 as a contribution to the celebration of the 225th anniversary of the Society's establishment in 1791, this meeting brought together prominent figures from every major branch of historical activity. Our guest list of fifty-seven included academic historians, archivists, documentary editors, a documentary filmmaker, an educational consultant, historical society administrators, librarians, museum professionals, community leaders, and members of the MHS family, including Board members, Fellows, and staff.

Drawing on a widespread albeit imprecise fear that the field of history, however defined, is in crisis, our guiding premise was that many of the problems we face span subfields to affect people who study and promote history in many different ways. In a keynote address, Pres. Jonathan F. Fanton of the American Academy of Arts and Sciences reassured us that "the past has a future," but this comforting idea did not assuage all the concerns when those in attendance met over the course of a day for a wide-ranging discussion of five questions: 1) "Is there a connection between academic history and the history the public consumes?" 2) "Are we doing the history we want to do?" 3) "What does history cost and how can we pay for it?" 4) "Does history matter?" and 5) "Where will we find the next generation?" For their help on an advisory committee, which met in April 2016 to consider the nature of the workshop, we are grateful to Lonnie G. Bunch, Charles F. Bryan, Joyce E. Chaplin, Louise Mirrer, Gordon

S. Wood, and Karin A. Wulf. Our thanks for taking leading roles at the workshop go to President Fanton and the five colleagues who facilitated program sessions: Catherine Allgor, John Lauritz Larson, Louise Mirrer, Woody Holton, and Marla R. Miller. In addition to all the others who participated in the workshop, we are grateful to the members of the staff of the Massachusetts Historical Society, who saw to all the arrangements for the program. A gift from Levin H. Campbell, Jr., helped to make both the workshop and the publication possible; we are grateful to him for his support.

The contributors to this volume all attended our workshop and agreed to respond to various of its themes through the essays presented here. We appreciate their participation as well as that of the Publications Department for handling the book's production.

WORKSHOP PARTICIPANTS

Catherine Allgor
Oliver F. Ames
Frederick D. Ballou
Rhonda Barlow
Thomas Birmingham
Debra Block
Ellsworth H. Brown
Levin H. Campbell
Levin H. Campbell, Jr.
Karen Cariani
Cinnamon Catlin-
  Legutko
Joyce E. Chaplin
Anna Clutterbuck-
  Cook
Elizabeth Deane
Christine A. Desan
Peter Drummey
D. Stephen Elliott
Paul J. Erickson

Dennis A. Fiori
Jamie Gass
Sara Georgini
Adam Goodheart
Elaine Heavey
Woody Holton
Marilynn S. Johnson
Katherine Kane
Martha J. King
Gavin W. Kleespies
John Lauritz Larson
Brenda Lawson
Ondine E. Le Blanc
J. Jefferson Looney
Stephen A. Marini
Sara Martin
Brendan McConville
Anne Craige McNay
Marla R. Miller
Christopher Minty

Louise Mirrer
Lisa B. Nurme
Thomas M. Paine
Patricia Puliafico
Richard Rabinowitz
Jan Seidler Ramirez
Miles F. Shore
Manisha Sinha
Megan Sniffin-Marinoff
Gretchen Sullivan Sorin
Patrick K. Spero
John Stauffer
Robert Townsend
William Tsoules
Katheryn P. Viens
Edward L. Widmer
Gordon S. Wood
Walter W. Woodward
Conrad Edick Wright